Caffeinated Ponderings

Caffeinated Ponderings

◆

On Life, Laughter and Lattes

Shana McLean Moore

iUniverse, Inc.
New York Lincoln Shanghai

Caffeinated Ponderings
On Life, Laughter and Lattes

iUniverse, Inc.

For information address:
iUniverse, Inc.
2021 Pine Lake Road, Suite 100
Lincoln, NE 68512
www.iuniverse.com

ISBN: 0-595-30377-3 (pbk)
ISBN: 0-595-66160-2 (cloth)

Printed in the United States of America

Contents

Acknowledgements

I would like to thank the following people from the bottom of my accelerated heart for the enthusiasm, support and coffee breaks they provided me while I put these caffeinated ponderings on paper:

To my girlfriends, both old and new, for enabling my addiction as we share our adventures over a hot cup.

To my brother, Matt, a fellow dreamer, for giving me noogies and a feisty edge early in life, and for giving me the sister I've always wanted in his wonderful wife, Meredith.

To my parents, Bill and Marcia, for the endless support and love that allowed me to view the world with humor and believe I could do anything I set my unconventional mind to.

To Tori and Taylor, my beloved daughters and writing fodder, whom I thank for the ever-increasing depth of my laugh lines, the soothing cuddles, and for not hating me when you eventually read this book.

To my husband, Russ, for his unyielding support of my schemes and dreams, for his amazing work ethic and commitment to our family, for the daily smiles and laughter.

To the people of Italy for thinking to grind espresso beans and combine them with steaming hot milk. Without your invention, I am nothing.

Preface

I wrote this book after countless hours of watching you. Whether our paths crossed in the grocery store, the coffee shop or as you petitioned for a restraining order against a stalker whose crime stopper's sketch bears an uncanny resemblance to me before I've showered, be sure that I've looked into your eyes and eavesdropped upon your conversations.

What I've concluded is that rich or Lottery-playing, fat or freakish, pasty white or the color of mocha, we're all in this together. We've acquired enough wisdom to weigh down our aging bodies, our children have given us a few more laugh lines than frown ones, and our spouses sometimes say things that should earn them a Darwin Award.

But you know what? I've also noticed that all of this is much more palatable when washed down with a professionally prepared cup of coffee.

My only request in sharing these observations with you is that you let me take cuts the next time our paths cross again while we're waiting in line for a latte. Cheers!

Introduction

WHY *IS* IT THAT…COFFEE IS LEGAL? (BUT I'M SURE GLAD IT IS!)

Whenever I reach a state of caffeinated nirvana, I stop to ponder how something that makes me instantly soothed and perky can possibly be legal. The mere idea that the Surgeon General could order those magical beans off the shelves and out of my life has me scheming towards the type of stock up that even Costco couldn't supply.

My fear is that these thoughts alone make me something of a textbook junkie. This is particularly clear when I confess to fantasizing about my next fix before the one I'm savoring has neither been finished nor gone cold. But before you go coordinating an intervention, please concede that there are benefits to spending time with a grown woman who indulges in such a deliciously harmless vice.

My husband sees the advantages so clearly that I'm afraid I might soon awaken with the tubes of a House Blend IV lodged in my arm as he tries to speed up my morning metamorphosis. For now, without the benefit of a slow drip of drip to jumpstart my day, he's stuck with a grumbling and disheveled woman who stumbles out of bed at the insistence of two annoyingly playful cubs. Before my eyes can even focus, our girls are ready to don their jazz pants and dance to the *Pure Disco* CD. At this hour, the music of my youth sounds much more like Pure Hell.

The actress in me does her very best to be impressed by their lead-footed jetés as I gulp down that first cup of the day. Within minutes…Yeah! Mom here is back in action. I'm ready to fix breakfast, pack lunches and, after a rare good night's sleep and an especially dark brew, even bust a few dance moves with the girls.

I refer to the euphoric time period after my first cup as B.C. (Blissfully Caffeinated). It is when the cobwebs clear and the feeling of hope returns to my normally happy and optimistic persona. This, my friends, is the most enjoyable yet dangerous time of day. You see, the day is new and the caffeine is pumping through and putting the spice back in this Spice Girl. Oh, the things that I am going to accomplish today! Sure the house is a mess, I have paper work to do and the refrigerator is empty. But why not invite some friends over for dinner? It's only 8:00AM and dinner is some ten hours away. No problem!

An hour later, I make the call and commit to the plan, only all of a sudden it doesn't seem so fun. The buzz is gone and has taken with it my delusions of grandeur. Why couldn't it have taken the chores instead? What have I done? I should know better than to make decisions while under the influence. Can I back out and claim temporary, java-induced insanity?

I know my addiction is worsening since the same high I used to get from one cup is now coming from two. Between you and me, when I'm in a real pinch of afternoon lethargy, I sometimes even push the envelope with a third cup. I do this well aware of the risk I run of sending myself into a Tasmanian Devil-like frenzy that will leave anyone within a three-house radius wishing they had a basement to shield them from the fallout.

I'm smart enough to realize that the physical rush that coffee brings me is too good to be healthy, but I'm hooked enough to do nothing about it. I'm comforted and validated by the solidarity I share with the nine or more similarly addicted individuals who wait in line like me for their sixteen ounces of wake-up. My only fear, as I tap my foot impatiently while awaiting my turn, is that one of the employees will single me out by calling me "Norm" and slide my usual order to the end of the bar. Only then will I concede that I've gone too far, and will sadly slink to step two in the recovery process.

But until I find myself with a reserved seat next to an all-knowing mail carrier at the coffee bar, or that dastardly Surgeon General deems my consumption illegal, I will continue to caffeinate. My reasoning is part selfish pleasure and part public service. Because the way I see it, at least eighty-four people, including my family, friends and the unsuspecting strangers whom I wave to with all five fingers as I let them merge onto the freeway, are counting on me to be full of life and energy. I assure you, dear reader, that a big 'ole cup-a-joe keeps me from letting them down and is, without question, the inspiration and creative force behind this book. I beg you to pour yourself a big one so that you may enjoy these pages in the spirit in which they were written.

1

Marital Mishaps:
I don't remember ordering a drip!

WHY *IS* IT THAT...MARRIED WOMEN NEEDN'T FEAR SHARKS?

I have always been a fearful woman. Whether the latest cause of my impending death would be an unleashed dog with enough foam on his mouth to top a large latte, or a shark about to mistake my figure-slimming black one-piece for a seal surrounded by jellyfish, I know when a vicious animal is out to get me. This is precisely why the creature that tops my list of things that inspire horror films is a newly certificated divorcée.

I'm sure my hierarchy of phobias would have been more traditional if it hadn't been for Julie. Most people, after all, would place gang bangers, home invaders and disgruntled postal employees in a far more dangerous category than they would a single woman working in Human Resources. The fools.

Like Freddy Kruger and Jason before her, Julie knew to strike when I was most vulnerable. She wasn't lurking outside with a dagger in the dark of night, but she may as well have. Julie struck, instead, when I was a frazzled and frumpy mother of a toddler and a newborn. And each day I sent my husband off to work while whining, wrinkled and haggard, she met him freshly showered and shined. I would have had a better chance against a machete.

My nemesis, Julie, revealed her name and playbook the day my husband sauntered in from work juggling his coat, laptop and a freshly baked cake. To a gal who counted dessert and its accompanying cup of coffee as the best coping mechanism for her current domestic state, this act should have warranted a passionate embrace of thanks. But before I could rid the man of the pastry, it occurred to me that this was a baked good of unknown origin: it didn't come to me in the telltale pink box nor in its cheap plastic counterpart. We were talking Saran wrap and a paper plate. This baby was homemade! And in the spirit of good storytelling, I will go so far as to say it had been made from scratch. Again, this observation would normally result in the type of passion that put me in my current frumpy predicament. But since my husband never mentioned a bake-off as one of his many obligations for the day, my Preda-dar sounded.

It appeared that Miss Julie from Human Resources baked my husband a cake because she knew he had been "having a hard time at work lately." Well, wasn't that *sweet* of her! I could only hope she meant this in only the most figurative of senses.

I took a deep breath and tried my best to stay loyal to my vow of jealousy-free living, but just couldn't help but ponder aloud some other measures she might take to cheer him up. Let's just say that I wasn't even considering a raise.

I think my husband will now agree that the correct response to my demonstration of marital vulnerability should have been something along the lines of "Honey, why would I want to be with anyone else when I can be with you?" Instead, my Romeo informed me that little Julie was too high maintenance and that she would never have him. Was the man driven home on a little yellow bus? How comforting it was to hear that the only thing keeping my husband from having an affair was the fact that the other woman wouldn't have him. In light of Miss Betty Crocker's actions, I might just beg to differ.

When his reply was met with a horrified gasp, the spin-doctor in him got into a gear only known by politicians. He claimed that the response I desired was a given and that he just wanted to allay my fears additionally with this extra tidbit of information. This man's got more spin per minute than my Maytag.

With his quick recovery time, my husband soon graduated to the big bus. And while he thinks that all is forgotten, I've been riding that bus much longer than he has. So while he thinks the kiss I plant on his lips as he walks through the door is just meant to welcome him home, I'm also secretly checking his breath for unknown sources of frosting. After all, I'm a woman who knows her marriage is far safer swimming off the coast of Key West at dusk than stepping into the office on any given workday.

Why *IS* it that...I can't relocate to Old England?

It seems that in all the books and movies set in the corseted days of England, you either were a maid or had one. If I could actually go back in time, I think I'd take those 50-50 odds. They sure beat the gig I've got going on at my house.

After all, it's tough on a girl to have to run the gamut between everyday house wench to lusty boudoir temptress...especially since the scent of bleach tends to linger. There's simply no amount of eau de toilette that can hide the fact that you've just cleaned one.

My fantasy of slipping back in time came to me as all the good ones do, when reeling with rage at one of my beloved husband's marital blunders. There I was, bent over the toilet, scrubbing while trying to keep my trendy but pesky layers of hair from blocking the view of my children's haphazard displays of urination, when my husband uttered a real nugget. "You clean the sink with the same sponge you use to clean the toilet?!" he declared with horror.

You would think he would have known better. Because to say that purifying the pot is not one of my favorite pastimes is about as understated as saying that our economy is not currently thriving. And, since I'm a girl never known to suffer in silence, my loathing for this chore is common knowledge. It is part of the illustrious group of global truths that no one but the Cliff Clavin-types bothers to question. The sky is blue. The workweek starts on Monday. You never talk to me when I'm working with a cleaning agent that will leave me with the skin of a reptile and the scent of an operating room.

Granted, a more happily domesticated woman might have appreciated the helpful, though unsolicited, advice. I'll tell you that this alley cat nearly scratched his eyes out. I held the bottle of Lysol with bleach up to the man's retinas and placed my hands on the trigger.

After he backpedaled with all kinds of sincere-ish statements about the health and well being of our family, I reminded him, a former science teacher, about the magical properties of bleach. He recalled that it killed germs, but seemed surprised to find out that the compound also helps husbands see things more clearly when aimed directly at their eyes.

I discovered that day that the mere threat of blindness by bleach is a guaranteed catalyst for an "Aha!" moment. As the flashbacks of our marriage unfolded before him, my man saw the morphing of his princess bride into the venom-spewing house hag who now stood before him. It was clear that I was a woman who had scrubbed one porcelain bowl too many.

His reaction to this epiphany wasn't exactly what I was yearning for. While my husband did confess to having bad timing, my fantasy was much more grand. I longed for him to grab the sponge from my hand and throw his cape dramatically to the floor to provide me with a proper exit. After all, he wouldn't want my delicate feet exposed to harsh chemicals that might cause fragile me to faint as I left to recover from the drudgery in the parlor. Or would he?

My only hope now is to lie awake at night, hoping that Michael J. Fox and his mad scientist cohort will swing by in the magical convertible for a trip back in time. Sure it's a coin toss. I would suffer the mother of all jetlags and could still end up with the same lot in life, with even fewer products at my disposal to scrub with. But there's an equal chance I could spend my days doted on by others while contemplating life's more profound issues, like whether my husband is shagging Lady Eldersby or whether my mother-in-law will succumb to smallpox.

Call me a dreamer, but I envision myself in the Old World lap of luxury. And even if something were to spill on it, I wouldn't be the one cleaning it up. But because the unforgettable smell of cleaning products would remind me of my former life as a peasant, I promise to be generous enough to share the secret uses of bleach with the poor wench who tends my manor.

WHY *IS* IT THAT…I'M TOO SEXY FOR MY CURLING IRON?

A tragic moment with my curling iron recently left me not only blistered, but also pondering the boundaries of sexiness. It all started with an unfocused moment of hair flipping that nearly seared the word "Conair" right across my neck. Now, some four days later, I actually wish it had. For if the logo had indeed transferred like a rub-on tattoo, I would have definitive proof that the wound I'm sporting is a bona fide curling iron burn and not some display of unwieldy machismo.

I understand why no one buys the "curling iron burn" excuse when you're sixteen years old and resurfacing from the back of your parents' steamy-windowed van. But when you're a thirty-five year old mother of two, with hair obviously in need of help from the very appliance you blame, you would think they'd believe you. It appears they do not. My husband was the first to offer a barb by proclaiming that I looked like I worked at Burger King. I found that comment initially hilarious, then slightly disturbing. Some happily married men apparently take mental notes about the workplaces of those who see more action in one shift than we did during year three of our marriage. Hmm.

The location of the branding made it impossible to hide on what I like to refer to as my swan-like neck. Not that I really needed to hide it, of course, because it was only a burn. Nevertheless, for a woman who preferred to look more like a customer of a burger establishment than an employee, if only given the two options, it was important to conceal what I could.

I refused to apply make-up because every girl over the age of fourteen knows that is the same as signing a confession. My parents would have grounded me for weeks! My only recourse, then, was to bundle up for the type of winter that a native Californian could only experience on vacation. I had hoped all the sweat from the increased circulation would lead to an early healing, though it didn't manage to happen before Saturday night's party.

Regretfully, when you are known to do your fair share of dishing it out, situations like this one ensure that you will be on the receiving end of heaping portions of abuse. Since the houseful of guests made it too warm to hide beneath several layers of high-necked garments, I wound up shedding them like a celebrity would a new partner in life until I wound up bare-necked and vulnerable to the observations of my "friends." Wouldn't you know it; the first to notice was the undiscovered fourth tenor. This man's voice knows how to fill a room. After a hearty "Shana has a hickey!" all eyes were on me as I blushed and stammered like I'd just been caught leaving my parents' van with a mouth like a precursor to a Chapstick commercial.

While the ribbing came from both men and women alike, it was clear that the girls were far more disgusted by the prospect of wearing the markings of sexual exploits. Many even came to my defense, citing their own experiences with the wand of shame. They all agreed that hickeys are so far past the line of decorum that, no matter what inkblot shape Rorschach intended them to come in; they all read "Scarlet S." And that's one "S" that never stands for "sexy."

The men made feeble attempts at agreement, but we couldn't help but notice that the sparkle in their eyes resembled the look of victory in the eyes of a hound that's managed to lift his leg in ownership on each of the neighborhood shrubs.

As happy as I was to contribute to the lively party banter, I plan on taking some precautionary measures to avoid becoming the target at our next social gathering. Since there's no other help for the paltry genetic grouping that resulted in this bad head of hair, I can't simply surrender my curling iron. I am just going to have to approach my morning grooming fully caffeinated and with the intensity of a surgeon. It sure beats the alternative of finding acceptance by earning minimum wage and wearing the unshakeable stench of the French fry station.

WHY *IS* IT THAT...I DON'T JUST BUY BEIGE?

These days I'm thinking that our military personnel and the average mother-of-the-groom have it all figured out. If you don't want to be shot at or, worse still, accused of upstaging the bride's side of the family, you ought to confine your purchases to subtle shades of beige. After all, the ability to blend in with the local landscape tends to keep our guys in uniform alive, and our family women from embarrassing themselves in a catfight at the altar. And if I were clever enough to apply the same principle to my attempts at sneaking a new wardrobe into our house, our family budget talks wouldn't be as heated as our south-facing sunroom on a three-digit day.

I blame myself for the disharmony. For if every shirt, short, dress and skirt I owned could be disguised and stored within the kids' sandbox instead of flaunting its vibrant newness from my open closet door, things would be much more civilized around here. I simply need to get over my attraction to color. Perhaps have the old cones removed from my retinas. See life through a dog's eyes—nothing too drastic.

In all beige, all the time, I could smuggle in hundreds of different garments that would fly right in under the enemy's radar. Surely he wouldn't notice an array of cargo pants and flak jackets that I would wind up resigning myself to, especially since my color choices would range only from Sahara Sand to Mediterranean Olive. I might as well give up my favorite stores for the local Army Surplus while I'm at it. That would bring the added bonus of a closet full of industrial strength fabrics that wouldn't even need to be dry-cleaned. Now we're talking true marital harmony!

In fairness to my shopping nemesis, though, he's actually no Saddam. He is my beloved partner in life who just can't comprehend the thrill a girl gets from debuting a new outfit. If only the brand spankin' new duds that leave me feeling radiant didn't leave him with an ire radiating throughout his coronary ventricles!

I fear that he may just be one ensemble away from planting a minefield that leads to the enemy's control center, otherwise known as my closet. The addition of one more hanger could just be the designated trigger to send the whole rod crashing down, moving us beyond our current "conflict" status and out into a declaration of war.

Fortunately, for the sake of domestic peace, a particularly volatile situation was defused a few weeks back when I met up with my hubby at a performance at our daughter's school. It might be relevant to disclose (though certainly does little to garner support for yours truly) that the show took place only a few days after a little chat about fiscal restraint. His argument included something about massive layoffs at his company, plummeting stock values and no bonuses in sight. Yadda-yadda.

So when I replay the situation in my mind, I now see that doing my best impression of a spring flower in my new little island printed skirt and its accompanying form-fitted red top might have been interpreted as an attempt to pick a fight. There I sat, chatting with friends in a metal folding chair, feeling simultaneously bold, guilty and pretty darned cute while awaiting my hubby's arrival to the show.

Once he got there, I signaled him to the seat I had saved. Just after we exchanged hellos, the woman on my husband's left (much to my horror) leaned over to ask me if this "darling little number" was the one I had mentioned splurging on at Ann Taylor. My only defense was to give her a bug-eyed stare and state with all the conviction of a lying politician: "Why, yes. This *is* the outfit. But I'm sure you're mistaken…I found it on sale at Target!"

I never said the enemy was a dummy. That's why my remark made him laugh first, and hardest. The first graders took the stage and gave me a chance to ponder the damage done. He *did* laugh…so how mad could he really be?

I'm still waiting to find out the extent of my man's wrath. Like any true enemy, he won't be announcing the exact time and place of his retaliation. Just in case there's still a possibility of a peaceful resolution, I am prepared to surrender my credit cards at a moment's notice. But until I can persuade him to schedule a summit on neutral ground, I will continue to approach my closet with utmost caution.

2

The Domestic Blend:
A bland, tired grouping of
suburban beans, ideal for
anything but a special occasion

WHY *IS* IT THAT...THE JONES' GRASS IS ALWAYS ONE SHADE GREENER THAN MINE?

Seven days out of eight I can ignore the fact that the Jones' grass is not only greener, but has achieved that obnoxious shade of Kelly that we humans only view favorably after a festive St. Patty's Day party. But something happens on day eight, and I don't think it has anything to do with the ale. I start seeing everything through emerald colored glasses. And while the neighbors' lawns fare well during my inspection, my own still never exceeds a lackluster shade of sage.

During my seven contiguous days of relative thankfulness and self-acceptance, I am at peace with the world. On day eight, however, I morph like a Ninja Turtle into that green-eyed monster who, because of some ocular deficiency in the beast gene pool, can't seem to see her own abundant good fortune. I must, instead, wish for what everyone else seems to have.

My earliest memory of suffering by comparison to a member of the Jones family is a Christmas I spent as a teenager. My mom overheard a conversation I had with a girlfriend in which I itemized each sock, pair of underwear and barrette I received that year. Mom was disturbed with the amount of detail I used until I recounted to her the haul my friend had collected from her own family. This friend also received socks, underwear and barrettes, but each was a set that matched the ten new outfits my friend, little Miss Barbie in-training, also received. Instead of being thankful for the many gifts I was given, I spent the evening pouting about this friend having received so much more. It was Christmas 1981, the year my internal ugliness was born.

The college version of Miss Jones was found in the beautiful, popular and perfect-bodied gal who was my best friend. Lucky me. My, oh my, was her grass ever greener! And her thighs were thinner, her boobs were bigger and the <beeeep> could eat anything she wanted. I could handle all of this most of the time because she was genuinely a lot of fun to be around.

It seemed as though each time I'd tire of being her booking agent, though, a nice little perk would present itself and keep me on the payroll. Because the truth is that when you're dining with the Pied Piper, there are usually a few choice leftovers. But wouldn't you know, every time the really prime ones approached, I'd hold my breath as they professed to me their love...for HER. In those moments, I felt pure empathy for Cinderella's ugly stepsisters who probably looked pretty good when she wasn't around ruining the beholder's point of reference.

This homely stepsister complex of mine (and a few flaws in my friend's personality that the boys never seemed to notice) eventually put an end to our friendship. I pride myself in having matured a lot since then. There may just be some room for growth, though, since my reaction to hearing this old friend was pregnant was to feel both genuinely happy and a wee bit nasty. Despite what you may be thinking, I'm not demented enough to wish her any real harm. But how about a few conspicuously placed stretch marks?

My eye for comparison became even more focused during my mid-twenties when a prospective suitor put me in my place. The charming Mr. Jones thought he was paying me a compliment by informing me that I was "refreshing" compared to all of the socialites he had dated. Apparently, this young man whom I looked at as my equal thought of me as his modern day Cinderella. The lad obviously needed some pointers from Walt Disney in learning how to unite two potential young lovers of such disparate social classes. Somehow I doubt the real Cinderella story would've had a happy ending if the Prince had sweet-talked her by saying the scent of cinders and bleach was like a breath of fresh air compared to that fussy French perfume all the princesses were wearing.

What young woman wants to feel that her boyfriend's friends, family and former love interests would eventually look at his time spent with you as slumming? Julia Roberts' character in *Pretty Woman* came to terms with it, but, frankly, she was a hooker and had little pride to lose. From this humbling experience, I learned that my love life would run more smoothly if I stuck with dating plebes, the card-carrying members of my own lowly caste. I would leave The Jones' to marry amongst themselves and bear freakish children.

But, sadly, even within my own socioeconomic circle, I occasionally find distant relatives of the Jones Clan. It's no wonder there are so many of them listed in the phone book...they're everywhere I go. Of course their house can be bigger, cuter or cleaner, but I sometimes even envy how they spend their time.

Whenever our street is littered with unfamiliar cars while roars of laughter and the scent of well-marinated barbecues spill over our fence, I feel a pang of envy that our neighbors might just be having more fun than we are. Once I pinpoint the house, I head straight to my address book to re-alphabetize yet another family under "J". Darned Jones'!

As pathetic as I am on the 8th day, however, don't think it hasn't occurred to me during my seven days of wisdom that I could possibly be a Mrs. Jones to someone observing me from a flaw-hiding distance. It may just be the way the sunlight hits the blades of grass when you look across the street through your own kitchen window that makes other people's grass seem so much greener. But if you're looking out yours on day eight, you might just catch me tripping a neighbor so I have a better chance of keeping up with the Jones'.

WHY *IS* IT THAT…DIRTY PANTS DON'T MAKE ME RANT?

There's simply no way to say this without looking like a Pollyanna. So I'll just spit it out and send you running to that barf bag you held on to after your last turbulent flight. *I don't mind doing the laundry.* There—I said it. But lest you envision me as a well-medicated house hag, I must add that I don't share the same tolerance for other tasks perpetually performed by us domestic goddesses. The mere mention of cooking for my hoard of temperamental eaters, for example, sends my blood pressure soaring to an altitude only NASA can equip a girl to handle.

And then there's the constant removal of filth. I'll tell you, consistency may be a desirable trait when attributed to a business environment, but when it refers to the cleaning up of the same toys, dishes and clots of toothpaste each and every day, we are talking about nothing less than a need for prescription medication. Any old over-the-counter anti-emetic, anti-depressant combination taken three times daily simply won't do. That's what they tell me, anyway. <Ahem>

But laundry is different. Each overflowing basket is a walk down short-term memory lane. Once I finally sit down amongst the rolling hills of darks, brights, mediums and once-upon-a-whites, I can't help but smile as I realize that the week's filth also serves as a week-in-review. Granted, some of those weeks are better off repressed, particularly those which involved potty training or plungers. The others, though, have highlights that really leave their mark, not only on our clothes, but also in my tender little heart.

The first items to stand out are those that boast the smell of fitness. It's really more of a stench, but it is one I am proud of. In addition to keeping me in an olfactory sort of touch with my European ancestry, the evidence of my workout reminds me to pat myself on my mildly toned back for finding the time to do something good for myself.

During my inspection, the jogging clothes steal the show by proving that even extra, extra dry is no match for the friction created by the frenzied union of fleshy arms and a torso. The shorts and tank tops from our weekend volleyball matches come in a close second. After a few days' incubation, the smell of sunscreen seems to help neutralize the once toxic vapors now trapped within the musty hamper. As several errant blades of grass spill from the pockets as I sort, I celebrate my tenacious side that just won't let that ball drop without a heroic attempt to put myself in a full body cast.

And though the opportunity is rare, I love running across the shirt my husband wore on our most recent date night. I savor again a civilized moment of uninterrupted conversation and professionally prepared food that is served without sippy cups and crayons. By the time I clean the shirt, the moment is over as we run about our mid-week tasks. But I do love to pause and remember why I married this creep who is getting home late and making me late for a meeting.

While reaching in to the next layer of the archaeological dig that is our hamper, I run across a sexy little number that has no business in there at all. Tisk, tisk. My children should do as I say and not as I do by putting that which was worn for under a minute right back in the drawer it came from. <*Blush*>

When sorting through the children's offerings, their blankies are what make me pause. It should, instead, be their pants because those pockets tend to contain treasures not imagined by the folks in engineering at the Maytag plant. I've cleaned too many precious stones that bare an uncanny resemblance to dirt clods and have laundered many a lip-gloss that leaves an oil spot on each garment within a three-shirt radius of the pocket that contained it.

The blankies, in contrast, have nothing to hide but themselves. We don't exactly confess that we even own the little sheaths, but are mighty particular about their state. Each time I sneak them away for a much-needed soak, my daughter complains that I've "washed the cuddles off." To keep the health department from intervening, I anticipate her adorably well-rehearsed response as I add blankie to the load…and then throw in a dash of bleach for good measure.

After the dryer completes its last rotation, it's time for the fold and put away. By now the chocolate stains from our spontaneous stop for ice cream are no longer in evidence and I've lost all sentimental attachment to the chore. There is, however, one final reward for doing the laundry since the seven consecutive loads have allowed me to harvest enough change and small bills to finance my next latte. Scrubbing the toilet will never give me any of that.

WHY *IS* IT THAT…EINSTEIN LEFT *ME* TO DISCOVER SOCIAL RELATIVITY?

My family recently moved to a beauty of a new town. And, due to the local Homeowners Reich, it's pretty well guaranteed to stay that way. The neighborhood lawns are as manicured as the nails of the ladies who write the checks to maintain them and, unlike the well-exercised thighs of their residents, the houses sprawl unapologetically. It's no surprise, then, that the public schools here boast testing numbers that would make you feel like a post-dot.com fool for paying to send your children for a private education…even when your posh home décor implies that you could.

The only thing that isn't down right pretty about this town is the fact that my family just barely got in. So "barely," in fact, that if there were Reich-sanctioned railroad tracks traversing the town, they would run right through my living room, putting my bedroom on the dreaded "wrong side of the tracks." So, if not for the hair on our highly mortgaged chinny, chin, chin (that's obviously in need of a salon treatment), we might just live in a town actually endorsed by our checkbook.

I'm not campaigning for a telethon to help me with my upper middle class plight. I just need time to adjust. Only time or the J. K. Rowling of all book deals can really help me now. But somehow, I feel that even a manicure could help ease the pain from my latest epiphany: when you move from a place where you were trotting along comfortably in the middle of the pack, it hurts like a leg cramp to be pulling up the rear like the winded fat kid in P.E.

I always assumed the principles of The Bell Curve could be applied to non-academic subjects, such as P.E. and general social hierarchy. You have the elite, the pack and the people to pity. It's a simple fact of life. But, now that my family has mortgaged itself into the western corner of a shiny new bell, that fine and useful tool of measurement is starting to hurt my feelings.

Now that I've moved to the west end of a bell, I've become an Einstein literalist. I want the term "relativity" to have everything to do with space and time, and nothing to do with zip code. Because back when I lived in the spacious body of a bell, I had plenty of company who felt as comfortable as I did in being average.

I was rarely exposed to people living on the respective edges since, frankly, the elite spent their days "doing" five-star lunches while the other extreme was busy serving it to them. My people pretty much made and ate their own peanut butter and jelly sandwiches. On the rare occasion I tired of my condiments and felt resentment for the elite, I just relished in the control I had over when the ringer would smack those East Enders for the sake of song.

With my new lot in life, I now know that West End girls do a lot of observing. I notice, for example, that the accessories I wear on the days I really have my act together have more of a Target twinkle than a Tiffany's one. My finally paid-off, five-year-old car also lacks the luster, scent and hood ornamentation of an East Enders'. Somehow, though, I still manage to get from point A to point B with nary a breakdown, at least with my car.

My newly fine-tuned eyes and ears recently honed in on a conversation that struck me like the rebound from an East End ringer. As I jogged along breathlessly after dropping my girls off at school, three girls passed me on their way to a neighboring middle school. As they passed one of the many grand homes, one girl innocently asked another if the waterfall in front of the house was the same one she had at her own home.

Well, if the girls assumed the snorting gasp that escaped my dropped jaw could be chalked up to my being like the winded fat kid in P.E., they were right on a couple of levels.

WHY *IS* IT THAT…CINDERELLA DIDN'T GET THE CASTLE?

I recently took my first stroll down Disneyland's Main Street USA, as a mother, and was pleasantly surprised to discover that the magic and excitement were nearly the same as I experienced during my own childhood…until I saw The Castle. It was an Ally McBeal moment, really, as I came to a screeching halt, complete with sound effects. How on earth did Sleeping Beauty wind up with Walt's main tribute? We can presume that all the princesses ended up with that kind of regal square-footage after being rescued from a mundane life by a dashing royal. So what is so special about Sleeping Beauty? I propose we rally around re-naming those digs after a more deserving princess.

Our country, founded as it was with a disdain for aristocracy, prides itself on the self-made man. So why not recognize a girl who at least paid a price for her address and tiara? Sleeping Beauty should never have qualified since she did nothing more than frolic in the forest and prick her noble little finger on a spinning wheel. I, for one, am not impressed.

Snow White's credentials aren't any better. Her résumé touts her as the fairest of them all, but even if we agreed with such a bestowal, should all the glory really go to a bubblehead of a gal who lets the scariest of strangers right through her front door? How do you explain *that* to your kids? Yeah, yeah. So she pays the price of slipping into a coma for doing so, but how much of a deterrent is that when one kiss brings her back to the few senses she possesses?

Then there's the Little Mermaid, a pretty-faced malcontent. She wants legs? I'll give her half the girth of mine, but not The Castle.

That leaves us with my pick, good 'ole Cinderelly. I feel the wench's pain daily while cooking, cleaning and enduring the demands of my own little Anastasia and Drusella. While entrenched in mindless scrubbing, I tend to fantasize about having my own little set of friendly mice scurrying about, trying to make sure I look acceptable before heading out to my life's version of a ball (read: potluck dinner). I say this, however, without knowing for sure if the dead rat I found in the yard last week met his demise while searching for the perfect sequin that would have transformed my sweats into something of a Gucci pantsuit.

And if I could only get a hold of just a little "Bibbidi Bobbidi Boo" to change my sexy station wagon into a delicate coach, and my sale-priced size eleven shoes into dainty glass slippers, The Castle could just as easily be mine. That is, of course, if I could be guaranteed that my Sasquatch-like dimensions would not force them to explode into shrapnel as soon as I practiced my first curtsy.

So if The Castle can't be yours or mine, since we weren't conceived in Walt's gifted imagination but, instead, in an icky-to-visualize moment of our parents' passion, I am forced to conclude that Cinderella is the next best choice. Sure she had the benefit of some magic, but she also endured the wrath of a stepmother who makes the Maleficent of all mothers-in-law look more like Flora, Fauna and Merryweather combined. And lets not forget that, at the end of the day, Cinderella's entire support group was nothing more than a pack of rodents that we modern day girls would have exterminated long before they had the chance to demonstrate their kindness and domesticity.

3

The Plight of an Aging Bean: Pick me before I'm compost!

WHY *IS* IT THAT…I'M ALREADY TOO OLD TO BE A GROUPIE?

I will never forget the details of my own personal (albeit horrendously shallow) tragedy that spurred the realization that my youth was not only passing…it had all but passed out. I really should have seen it coming, what with a husband, two children, a mortgage payment and a station wagon. But for some reason, I spent eleven years thinking that, despite my facial fault lines and very adult responsibilities, I was but a young filly.

The first brick on my path to enlightenment was set after I told my second year Spanish students to hurry and buy tickets for the Enrique Iglesias concert that my friends and I would be attending. Please bear in mind that many of these youngsters, at that time, had never heard of Enrique, much less his eye-candy of a father, Julio, who melted my own mother's heart but who has already exceeded his shelf-life as a sex symbol. My announcement, therefore, was made for a small audience since the majority of these students, despite my efforts, still can't seem to comprehend why anyone would bother singing or speaking in a language other than English. (And we hoped the "Ugly American" was just an international myth!)

The day of the event arrived and we teachers excitedly entered the venue and took our seats. As Enrique entered, the girls (and I do mean girls) went wild! The path to my awareness neared completion as I realized that I, too, might have rushed the stage with a frisk-me sort of stance a decade or so ago. But at my current level of maturity, I thought it enough to swoon in my chair like a dirty old woman. This feeling was magnified when Enrique brought one of these boy-toys up from the audience and sang a romantic little medley while his mouth stood only about six inches away from hers. I'm sure that every female (and perhaps a male or two) in that audience left the show that night with a secret little fantasy that Enrique had chosen her to sing to that night.

Imagine, then, the profound emotional damage that I suffered in class on Monday after I shared with my students how much I enjoyed the music. As the students were leaving, one girl pointed to a poster that decorated one of the classroom walls and asked if it was a picture of Enrique. When I verified that it was, in fact, him, she replied that he wasn't very cute. I felt it was my duty, as one who claims to be a purveyor of enlightenment, to give the poor, lost girl an education on beauty and proceeded to show her a picture from one of his CDs. She whipped her head from his picture to my face, and declared with an innocent sort of horror that I could be Enrique's mother. The blow nearly knocked me from my feet while simultaneously shattering the weekend's fantasy. Somehow it isn't quite as sexy to imagine Enrique singing that love song to the likes of his own mamá! Cut the landscaper a check, the path is complete!

My girlfriends and I laughed about this whopping blow to my ego (they much more than I) and comforted ourselves with a simple mathematical equation. Thank God we all hit puberty much later than the requisite age of eight and really couldn't have given birth to that fine specimen of a man. By our calculations, we have been spared for at least another seven years. At that point, chronologically speaking, anyway, the newest twenty-something heartthrob could reasonably have passed through our birth canal. Our moral challenge will then be to evaluate whether the risk of being perceived as a pedophile outweighs the potential for a few moments of lustful reverie. If that doesn't just extinguish any hope of a good fantasy, I don't know what would!

WHY *IS* IT THAT…A ZERO MAKES A FASHION HERO?

I'm not exactly the poster child for a public school education since mine gave me little more than a nervous twitch that starts to flutter whenever someone references an important piece of literature. Yet somehow, despite my lack of exposure to many of the classics, and a brilliantly choreographed avoidance of any subject requiring the creation or comprehension of formulas, a few key concepts stand out in my muddled mind.

Perhaps it's a blonde thing, but my earliest classroom discoveries are those that remain the most vivid in my adult mind. And to think those memories were formed when I came by my hair color naturally! I may be a formula-phobe who can't back this up with the credentials of a chemist, but I'm thinking the trouble may just lie in the bleach. All I know is that once my hair became more man-made than God-given, my memory for facts became, shall we say, blonde.

The things I know for sure, then, are the very same that inspired the book *Everything I Need to Know I Learned in Kindergarten*. I assure you that the title alone brought me a great sense of relief and validation. For it was in kindergarten, somewhere between a chorus of "B-I-N-G-O" and a passionate session of finger painting, that I gained an understanding for the evil number, zero. Zilch. Nada. Nothing.

The meaning of the empty, oxymoronic "number" became clear in a single lesson that didn't require a pencil, paper or even a credentialed teacher. Apparently, if I brought three cookies for my recess snack and Johnny, the big fat bully, took them all away, I was left with nothing. Concept mastered. Memory ingrained.

And though I never needed this mathematical principle to be reinforced due to its dramatic introduction, good 'ole zero kept sneaking itself in to draw attention to my loss. Have four friends; get caught talking behind their backs over something more Petty than the rock star Tom himself; zero friends. Have five dollars of allowance saved; spend it all on a stupid snow globe while on vacation; zero money to go to the movies with the friends who finally forgave me. Have plans for the weekend; bring home bad grades; zero chance of going out—ever.

Since I always had more than a mild disdain for zero, imagine the dog head tilt of confusion I displayed the first time I ran across a size zero in the pant rack at my favorite store. Fortunately for me, this discovery didn't happen until I was in my twenties, when I was just a mere ten years from the verge of accepting myself for who I was. Hats off to mom for protecting me from a horrific retail reality that would have robbed me of the shard of self-esteem that I clung to, bloody hands and all.

Of course I had known since junior high, from the very first purchase of *Chemin De Fer* jeans that made me not just *tres chic* but *tres Jimmy Dean*, that when it came to pant size, smaller was better. But I was supposed to aim for zero? Sure there was a zero *in* my size, but since the moment I made my debut in the junior department there was always another digit cuddling up to the left of it.

I was baffled. Could there actually be a female whose waist size matched that of my old Barbie, yet had the inseam of an actual human? And if said woman fit into a pant size labeled "zero," did she not suffer the same plight as my stolen recess snack and cease to exist? Ruh? It was going to take more than Scooby Snacks to figure that one out.

But after ten years of channeling my inner Nancy Drew, I finally cracked the case. Since the only zeros walking around in the real world are those serving as placeholders for sizes that come in multiples of ten, it may be safe to deduce that these gals and their exciting lifestyles are like the ghost story mysteries my mentor, Nancy, used to solve.

In this case, the nefarious human plot behind those ghostly apparitions that haunt us until we hate our thighs is simply a conspiracy between the Magazine Airbrushers Union and the jean manufacturers to hurt the feelings of the average gal who likes her cookies.

Armed with that realization, I can now pity the waify silhouettes that show me how the latest fashions are supposed to look. Lord knows they have *zero* chance of savoring real world delicacies like avocado, bacon fried in its own fabulous fat, or an extra-large blended mocha with whipped cream.

WHY *IS* IT THAT…RUNNERS' THIGHS MAKE ME SIGH?

I'm always careful to declare that I'm a jogger, not a runner. It's all about credibility, really. For, a real runner would only need to give me a shallow once-over to know the truth anyway—because the thighs tell no lies.

From the vantage point of my hearty family tree, the willowy speedsters who gallop along on legs that closely resemble a set of gangling arms, are freakish enough to qualify for permanent membership in Cirque de Soleil. They should feel quite at home among the pretzel people who have bodies that twist and contort more than a twenty-ounce bag of Rold Gold.

Come to think of it, the runners are simply another variety of the pretzel species: namely, the fat-free sticks. And darn it if that doesn't leave us jogger-types to claim the bulky "rod" variety as our own! Despite the name, the rods are hardly as sexy as their more petite and curvaceous counterparts. Yet on the positive side, they're still leagues more glamorous than their sister snack food, the potato chip, with all its couch-y connotations.

The legs on those sticks look like they might actually need to be formally introduced to one another as they glide by in those sleek micro-shorts. We hearty joggers could compete with their gait if not for our pesky conjoined thighs that are about as good for speed as Keanu Reeves was for the movie.

Many of us with Siamese thighs secretly long for an operation that will give "the girls" a separate existence. The fear of becoming both shallow and bankrupt prevents us from booking the procedure. Instead, we risk becoming an example to the contestants of *Survivor* for how to start a fire with nothing more than the flesh between your femurs, and just start trotting at a sloth's pace.

The girls are like a pair of squabbling sisters, continually fighting over who gets to go first. Their struggle causes quite a ruckus and, frankly, a not so insignificant rash. So while it would be fun and sporty to dress like a real runner, those modern-day Dolphin shorts just can't offer enough of an inter-appendage buffer to those of us who have nothing short of a love affair with snack foods.

Let's be honest. It isn't very attractive to see a pair of shorts who've surrendered their duty of individual leg containment by heading northward to avoid involvement in such a heated skirmish. To avoid such ugliness, I recommend donning the ever-sexy biking short whenever the mood to induce sweat strikes. Sure. You'll never be featured in *In Style* magazine for wearing cycling shorts when having no intention of mounting a bike, but they're the ideal solution for both a girl's pocketbook and her psyche. Just think of the money you'll save when you needn't buy talcum powder and Desitin to combat that chafing! And your self-esteem will soar when you're never asked again to explain the principles of physics by demonstrating the ascent of your running shorts.

Once the girls are contained and you've done the rest of your pre-flight preparation, you're ready for take off. The right shorts hit the optimum cruising altitude, somehow aware that any excessive climbing could result in difficulty in breathing for the unsuspecting passerby who happens to catch the site without protective eyewear.

Since you've selected your own in-flight music, the journey will be as pleasant as possible for a vehicle last fueled at Starbucks. After what feels like a slew of interminable songs that seemed far more energizing when listened to from the couch, it's finally time to prepare for landing. Just as you begin to congratulate yourself for the rash-free, sustained aerobic activity, having scored yet another victory against the evil desire to stay seated, one of the sticks manages to whoosh by and scare you to death. Without heavy breathing or the sound of whistling fabric between their thighs, you never know they're coming!

They're just lucky that you're too exhausted to retaliate for both the startle and the demonstration of prowess by pulling the trigger on that canister of pepper spray or unleashing your vengeful inner dialogue, which comes out sounding like a rap song due to all the post-workout panting.

> Runners' thighs, they make me sigh
> But just like the tortoise and the hare,
> My joggers' thighs will get me by.
> I'm slow, but I'll get there.
> (Huh-huh-huh!)
>
> On my bones there is some meat
> There ain't too much on yours
> My taste buds they enjoy some treats
> Your body's just beggin' for more.
> (Huh!)
>
> On your runs you go so fast
> Past me, you blaze right by
> In your race I come in last

But in mine, I win the prize.
(Huh-huh-huh!)

Psst. Pass me my Krispy Kreme.

WHY *IS* IT THAT…MORE MEN DON'T SUE VICTORIA'S SECRET?

You needn't look to 34th Street to find a modern-day miracle. But be prepared! If your standard for defining one includes only the mere acts of turning water into wine, parting the Red Sea or walking on water, the bar is about to be raised. For, I am talking about the unbelievable feat of lifting and padding a woman's chest to hoist her from A to C faster than a kindergartener can tell you which letter goes between them. Yep. Victoria's Secret named its Miracle Bra aptly, and my husband's testimony will be quoted in the history books for generations to come. I'm just lucky that we said our vows and sealed the deal with a "home run" before I started to fill both my lingerie drawer and my shirts with that pricey little contraption. After all, I wouldn't want to be sued for misrepresentation.

The first moment of physical intimacy you share with your mate is nerve-wracking enough, but when you know you could be accused of deceit as he slides into second base, it's got to be enough to make you want to pop a Xanax. Again, I can only imagine this anxiety since I got married B.M.B. (Before Miracle Bras). These were the days when a shallow man could judge a book by her cover. What my hubby saw on my tiny little shelf was, sadly, all he got. Come to think of it, though, it might not have been a coincidence that he started to visit the optometrist shortly after we made things official. But by then it was too late. He'd lost his receipt, torn off the cover and was genuinely smitten by more than my measly table of contents. Poor chap!

Our babies eventually arrived and proceeded to suck what little I had right out of my being. Lucky for me, the timing couldn't have been better to be a deflated little life raft. Victoria's Secret, the creator of every man's favorite catalog, was blossoming into a major retail contender, complete with prime time commercials. Victoria was anything but hush-hush about her unmentionables! Each of her ads boasted a well-fed Miracle Bra that forced me to gawk, envy and purchase one in every color. As I learned to tuck and arrange my flesh so that the magical contraption could levitate and pad me beyond pre-partum heights, I always had the same guilty thought: without the benefit of a crack marketing team, wouldn't many of Victoria's divine creations simply be called prosthetics?

Nevertheless, I'm still a believer. I recently returned to the pearly pink gates with my three-year-old daughter in tow, my mind wide open to any type of magical or divine intervention. The saleswoman perceived my urgency (either because of the puckering of my undergarment or the actions of my preschooler) and was eager to help. Before we could reach the Miracles, though, she diverted me to the celestial new gel-filled version. My first reaction was to gasp at the costly, self-standing structure before me. Then it occurred to me that if I wore one of those, I would be forever haunted by the lyrics of *You're so vain*. Did I really want to be sure that Carly's song was about *me*!?

As I pondered the consequences to my self-image, my daughter, in a rare moment of helpfulness, insisted on carrying the contraption to the dressing room for me. She staggered off like The Hunchback with the heavy cargo that was to become my destiny. Once I was secured and fastened, I took a look at my cheating self in the mirror. I tried to look subdued in order to spare my daughter a shallow memory of her mother, somehow managing to keep the full-blown choral version of "Halleluiah!" to myself.

I had always vowed I would never go under the knife to rectify the genetic mutation that left me with a cup-size disproportionate to the rest of my beefy body parts. But with no blood, no scars, no social stigma and a buy-one-get-one-free sale, what *was* a girl supposed to do? I assure you that my sweaters are still wondering what happened on that fine day at the mall.

But like anything that seems just too good to be true, there are risks to owning a Miracle Rack. For starters, I strongly suggest that you wear an everyday standard issue when going to Weight Watchers or your annual physical exam. The staff will usually understand if you want to take off your shoes before weighing in, but bra removal is sure to raise some eyebrows, and send your mammary glands south enough to land you a National Geographic cover shot. Additionally, you must avoid sharp objects at all costs. Once your children are older than three, it's a bit difficult to pass off any pectoral secretions as lactation. And finally, should your wedding vows not be durable enough to last a lifetime, there's always the chance that a jury of your peers will see the real you as Exhibit AA.

WHY *IS* IT THAT…I REALLY WOULDN'T RATHER BE SHOPPING?

We've all seen cars with license plate frames boasting that the finely clad driver within would "rather be shopping." I used to consider honking my horn in agreement and following them on their next wallet-emptying outing until I pondered how my credit card wouldn't be the only thing I would be maxing out.

The stitching on the fitted pants I would inevitably try on in a moment of optimism would certainly be feeling the pressure, as well. If those same pants could talk, I'm sure they would feel compelled to ask what all the hype is about Jennifer Lopez's backside. After all, they could attest that their threads worked harder at keeping me from busting out of mine than any pair of her designer duds would ever need to.

Couple that with the frustration of trying to confine my squirrelly young children who try to get an eyeful of other shoppers brave enough to bare all as these little voyeurs peek under the dressing room wall, and I'm not sure why I bother at all. Don't think I haven't tried everything, including threats and bribery, to get their cooperation. I end up wrestling them and the latest pair of pants made by designers who are constantly reducing the space within a garment that claims to be a size 10. The problem is with the cut, right?

Last I heard, the A.M.A. was confident that symptoms of depression and high blood pressure were meant to be avoided; not sought after voluntarily. Yet, nevertheless, I must sometimes forgo their warning and take the emotional and physical risk of going back to the mall.

The real kicker is that when I've survived the chaos and actually found something suitable, the retail rush is always fleeting. It wanes the moment I hit the driveway and realize I must now declare my purchases to my in-house Customs Department. I feel a bit like O.J.'s lawyers as I concoct an opening statement that even I don't believe in order to defend the "necessity" of a fourth pair of black pants that hardly even seem worthy of the fanfare.

So until my children are old enough to be left at home, and both my budget and the fit of my pants are a little looser, I will have to accept that shopping is not what it used to be. The days of visualizing myself in the pages of *Seventeen* magazine as I whiled away the hours and my father's hard-earned money at the mall, are a distant memory. I have to accept, too, that the thrill I got from buying my first pair of Dolphin shorts, a la Richard Simmons, the dazzling gold lamé headband that matched my glittering flats and belt, and the off-the-shoulder *Flash-*

dance-inspired top that made me feel like singing "What a feeling!" will not soon be replicated in my present-day visits to the mall.

Alas, shopping (like restaurant dining and hotel stays) is an activity that was much more enjoyable before those diaper-wearing, nap-needing, feed-me-now-or-I-will-drop-dead creatures became my constant companions. Before their arrival, both the budget and the amount of leisure time dedicated to such deliciously selfish pursuits were decidedly beefier, while the body parts I had to dress were relatively scant. Now, I'm afraid, those proportions are reversed. The fat deposits have shifted from my free time and have clung for dear life to my thighs. And while the term "scant" no longer applies in a physical sense, it is the best way to sum up our bank balance and unscheduled time on the calendar.

So I really can't, in good conscience, accessorize my car with a declaration that would define me as an exclusive shopper. It just wouldn't be a truthful representation of the driver within. Then again, I could channel my inner "Dream Team" and add some tiny disclaiming script at the bottom that read: "provided that my bank balance were bigger, my @$$ were smaller, and my children were staying home with my mute husband."

Fortunately for me, I've also discovered that I rarely mourn the loss of every girl's favorite pastime when I take a moment of my time, and a duty-free amount of pocket change, to find a similar legal high by nipping into my favorite coffee shop. For now, at least, "I'd rather be sipping a latte."

WHY *IS* IT THAT…EXERCISE ISN'T A FOUR-LETTER WORD?

Don't get me wrong; endorphins do rock. Sadly, though, the only way to release them by a healthy means requires a significant physical expenditure that I am often too tired to pursue. Were I a raver or a Hollywood celebrity, I could find the same high by prescription or from the basement of an un-credentialed chemist. But no, I am just an average woman who finds her guilty euphoria at the espresso bar and her healthy one **post**-workout.

The more athletic of you may feel this sense of jubilation while exercising, but most of us more sedentary types don't feel any pay-off until the fat lady's gig is so far over that she's back home on the couch…where we wish we could stay. We see you run past us with an expression of exhilaration that we find nauseatingly perky when we are just hoping our workout doesn't reach its end with a call to 911.

Like all of you, I have plenty of excuses not to bother. Two weeks per month are easy to rationalize what with P.M.S. and, subsequently, M.S. The week after that flies right by as I focus my energy on mending fences for all the atrocities committed during "that time of the month." During that one special week when my relationships are in sync and those hormones are no longer an easy scapegoat, I am forced to look for a host of external reasons to forgo Nike's advice, and simply not do it. The weather is an easy target since anything above or below seventy-three degrees just doesn't work for me. Then there are those tiny other little obstacles that get in the way like work, household maintenance and spending time with your family.

When I run low on excuses (or cannot fasten a single pair of pants), I resign myself to a ride on our stationary bike. It would be a good workout if I didn't need to jump off every ten minutes to prevent computer hacking and/or a sibling brawl. A few more rides and I may just have mastered the art of talking down the perpetrators before the actual crimes are committed. Perhaps I can parlay these skills into a brilliant career in law enforcement once my chicks leave the nest. For now, these workouts are even more exhausting mentally than they are physically. I know that my body is moving and my heart is pumping aerobically, but so is my darned blood pressure.

It's no accident that the mood to move overcomes me more often on the weekend. After all, daddy is home and ready to play with his girls, so mommy here can escape virtually unnoticed. If forced to be totally honest, I'm not sure I crave the workout as much as I just need a good excuse to be alone for an hour. I shut the door to responsibility, turn on my music (no Barney or Sesame Street CDs allowed) and shake my gelatinous groove thing.

I resurface stinky and ugly, but also somewhat proud and rejuvenated. I might just do this again tomorrow…or the next time we experience spring weather when my husband has a day off and I am feeling at peace with the world despite the tight pants…and can afford to spend the next day in bed.

WHY *IS* IT THAT…WE RARELY EVER FEEL OUR AGE?

Sure there are moments when the knee goes dodgy, the 'ole back won't quite straighten or too many people have recently called me ma'am, but during my caffeinated hours, I feel as prime as any rib that costs top dollar in a fine restaurant. So on the average day, with the cooperation of my bones, joints and our town's waiters, as well as a successful avoidance of the latest sounds and styles on MTV, I would swear I could be a card-carrying member of Generation X. Sometimes even Y! Since my problems are few and can be cured, respectively, by Advil, a deaf ear and a remote control, I'm sure I have yet to gain your sympathy. Please be aware, though, that not feeling your age can lead to the ailment of near fatal temperatures in the facial region, usually accompanied by a temporary lack of oxygen and a general sense of mortification.

For that reason, I'm considering carrying around a mirror with me at all times to ward off future discomfort and humiliation. When you catch me sneaking a look, please do not scoff at what you assume is vanity. Well, there may be an occasional check to make sure I'm still capable of coloring between the lines, and another on the lookout for the occasional misdirected sprout, but my main purpose will be a reality check.

My problem, you see, is that I still think I am a kid. I actually have some of the pimples to support my delusion, but, fortunately, am not plagued with the baggage of wondering whether or not I am popular enough. I think a quick peek at my reflection might just remind me that the wrinkles I have accumulated from years of laughter, and what now would be described as suicidal amounts of sun worship, are there to remind me that I really am no longer one of *them*.

You know, the whippersnappers. The ones you mistakenly address as your peers until they bring up a pop culture reference from their wonder years that means as much to you as a page of hieroglyphics. If you haven't quite mastered your poker face, you will then be asked the defining question: "*When did you graduate?*" It is then that you can be sure that this hobbledehoy is not even in the vicinity of your ballpark age-range. Heck! With this discovery alone, you may be assured that their game is more likely to boast Barry Bonds while yours feels closer to Babe's.

If I had done a reflection inspection just prior to the birthday party I attended last weekend, I might have prevented the near fatal flush. Just after cake disbursement, a familiar woman walked into the kitchen. I recognized her immediately, but couldn't remember her name or how we had met, which, by the way, should certainly have been a warning sign of my chronological decay, in and of itself. But I did still have enough Nancy Drew in me to need to discover our connection. I was sure she was someone I had not seen in many years, so I thought it best to ask if we had gone to the same high school. When that left me no closer to solving the mystery, we then moved on to names. As soon as I stated my maiden name, the woman before me morphed into a wee lass as she declared excitedly that I had been her high school Spanish teacher. My only thoughts at that moment were, *Call 911. An elderly woman has fainted and is now experiencing shortness of breath and a shattered sense of denial.*

And in case you are wondering, I wasn't one of those child-geniuses who began her career at age sixteen. Nope! I had this poor gal by at least a decade but never considered that she could be anything less than my peer. I had obviously forgotten the harsh reality of my morning make-up session as I assumed the smooth and taut countenance I was addressing was receiving one of similar caliber.

Mirror, mirror on the wall, who is the most deluded one of all? I am pretty sure I know the answer so I think I will unfasten that mirror from the wall and drag it around with me at all times…just in case I should forget my place on the chronological totem pole again.

4

Girlfriends:
Sugar and spice and all things
nice (like caramel and whipped
cream!)

WHY *IS* IT THAT…GIRLFRIENDS COST LESS THAN THERAPY?

If it were necessary, wouldn't you pay a premium price for the friendship of a treasured gal pal? I would do so with no questions asked because I know it would be a better investment than any Blue Chip stock. Instead of cutting a hefty check to a cerebral third party who listens coldly to my woes, I make the painless investment in a sister.

I suppose if I were to calculate the total amount spent on gifts and outings and even went so far as to affix a dollar amount to the time invested in the friendship, therapy might be the more fiscally sound option. Come to think of it, though, anyone who thinks of relationships in those terms needs a professional around to write their prescriptions.

Most of us girls who are blessed with true friends treasure the time and money spent in their company. The depletion of these two relished resources while in the company of a girlfriend is like ordering your favorite coffee drink with nonfat milk…it erases all the guilt!

Our girlfriends are the few cherished souls that completely understand our deepest fears and sorrows, as well as our greatest moments of pride and victory. While a man can come in as a close second by sympathizing with many of our emotional reactions, he cannot truly empathize with many of our feelings.

Take, for example, the feeling of panic that overcomes the less naive of us when we find ourselves walking in a deserted public area. Would anyone even hear us if we screamed? On a hot summer night, have you ever argued with your husband about leaving the first-story windows open? I, for one, would rather be sweaty than dead! While my husband respects my paranoid pleas (probably to avoid hysteria), my women friends are the ones who can truly understand this fear of vulnerability.

These girlfriends are also the ones who truly share my glee in the more superficial accomplishments of finding the perfect throw pillow that helps give my family room that Country French look I am trying to achieve, or the elation of hitting the retail jackpot by finding a knock-out dress that is both flattering and on sale.

If I still haven't convinced you to give up your spot on the proverbial couch for a date to a chick flick, please consider your girlfriends' credentials. Your long time friends' advice comes with far more than a PHD; it comes with a complete knowledge of who you were back then, who you are now and, hence, a clear understanding of why you are doing this cockamamie crap that has you in need of therapy in the first place.

Purge your soul to someone who not only knows your history but also lived many parts of it with you. Who better to discuss your issues of confidence and trust with than the same friend you sobbed to when little Eric Luselipps broke up with you and told the whole freshman class that you "kissed like a marshmallow"?

Some of my girlfriends go so far back that I liken my comfort with them to the feeling I get when I wear my old college sweatshirt. That old girl has survived international travel and eight different moves. Sadly, though, her adventures are starting to show. I hesitate to wash her since I know that each spin cycle will take a year of life off my 'ole buddy.

Just like my sweatshirt, my home fries and I are beginning to look a bit more like the lunch rush's leftovers. Our skin and muscles, which used to rival the tautness of a freshly filled helium balloon, are looking more like day two now, with the onset of shrivel.

We console ourselves by knowing that many of these creases are due, in part, to our endless summers of sun tanning in our backyards while freshly lubed in baby oil. We can be sure, too, that many of our laugh lines can be attributed to years of uncountable giggles and belly laughs that were often glamorously accompanied by snorts.

Though our hectic lives don't allow us to keep in touch with old friends as often as we would like to, the same level of comfort is there whenever we do. As our families and careers take center stage, our conversations and visits can become sporadic and short-lived. But a real friendship can withstand this and more. After all, we made it through the high school years and all of their inherent traumas that might have been responsible for the first divots in what are now our frown lines.

These days, though, our conversations are full of laughter and support, and are totally devoid of melodrama. None of us, thankfully, has felt compelled to appear on Jerry Springer to announce that we are sleeping with our best friend's husband or secretly have the hots for one of our gal pals. We are just a bunch of girls who appreciate how lucky we are to have a wealth of good memories and an openness to share our current lives, which allows our friendship to remain steady despite our geographic separations, diverse professions and variety of life stages.

And that, my friends, does more for me than any office visit—more than a therapist, beautician, or even a barista.

Why *IS* it that…no one places 'friend wanted' ads?

"SWF (with emphasis on the S) looking for partner in crime with whom to share laughter, tears, thigh loathing and shopping secrets. I'll know you're the one if I want to share my cherished latte with you."

If you have ever been a transplant or have had your girlfriends leave you to feel transplanted in your own town, please tell me you have felt my pain. When my last local girlfriend was packing her boxes to move out of town, we joked about finding me a replacement for her. Our final outings together turned innocent playgrounds into virtual meat markets of potential partners. Once she left, I actually stooped to using my beloved children as the decoys to drum up some conversation.

While I met many nice people, amongst the slew of cynics wielding pepper spray, none had that special spark that let me know she would be a soul mate. I spent about thirty days getting used to having all of my friend fixes injected by phone, which was certainly better than going cold turkey, but left me lonely for the eye contact and supportive hugs of a real friend.

Fortunately for me, the Big Guy realized that mine was a quick problem to solve since the health and happiness of my family and far away friends were already in check. All he needed to do was place the right woman in my path, and I would be able to take over from there.

I never suspected that the answer to my prayers would be just a few steps away in the new neighbors that would be moving-in any day. I must confess that I especially did not expect to find her there when I learned that a "nice, young English family" had bought the house. Yawn! "Tea and crumpets anyone?" Stereotype number 117 popped into my mind and brought me a clear example of their family's conversations: "After you." "No, no, after you." While this newest addition to my circle of friends is, in fact, extremely polite, she is so very much more than that. Thanks, Big Guy!

When reflecting upon how amazing it is that Jackie and I became such good friends in less than one year, I realized that we both possessed the four essential elements that are necessary to form a tight bond quickly. If you are feeling the need to recruit new girlfriends into your own circle, please grab a pencil and paper at once and write down my new acronym: ANOD. Once you know what each letter represents, I urge you to wear a baseball cap or t-shirt on your next local outing that reads: *Gimme A NOD!*

When you see a woman checking you out while nodding her head, you will know that she, too, possesses the N, which, my sisters, stands for NEED. Early in your conversation, however, please rule out the possibility that she is checking you out for more carnal reasons. Once that has been ruled out, your bobbing heads will have revealed that you are two people who are actively seeking a new friend. That ought to help speed things up.

If you are ever in a situation in which you are the only one possessing the N, do not fret because this need not rule out friendship. Just realize that it will take much longer to establish that closeness if the girl you have picked-up already has someone with whom to share her stories and secrets.

The big O is not the kind that you have with your husband, nor is it what he and the guys joke about us girls doing for each other when they feel threatened by our spending too much time together. We girls are just looking for *OPENNESS* in our girlfriends: someone who is quick to pocket the small talk and get down to the sharing of real life pain and joy. We want to know her secrets and for her to know ours, not just because we want to know all the gossip (please admit, though, that we do enjoy it) but because we really want to know her. As much as we possibly can, we want to make up for what we are lacking in history with this new partner in crime.

Think about your friendships and see if you can come up with D, more like a lack of D. So that you won't scan downward to cheat, I will leave it in lower case letters. Tricky me! It is something that we don't always share with our old friends, but it is essential with new ones. With our limited amounts of time and energy to expend in the creation of a new friendship, a lack of geographical *distance* is more than a plus…it is practically a requirement. It is certainly much easier to figure out if you hit it off with someone when you can't avoid running into her!

That leaves us with, perhaps, the most crucial and challenging element in the equation for bonding: *AVAILABILITY*. Between work, time with our spouse and our children's activities, there isn't much left over to put into a new friendship. If you feel that there is a mutual connection, you can make friendship happen, but it has to be a priority. Before you decide not to call her back because of your hectic life, remember that sharing your daily life experiences with a girlfriend allows the selfish young girl within you to come out and sing, dance and play…and it makes you feel whole. Realize that you don't benefit anyone by just being a wife, mother or employee. Please find the time to spend with your new friend, and you will see that your homemade drip coffee will start tasting like a mocha!

Once you have found someone with compatible *ANOD* scores, I suggest that you and your new friend start small with your outings. This way, shock waves won't start sinking the family boat. The first week you can go out for coffee, another time to a quick lunch and, eventually to the mall to pursue a retail rush. While you are out and about, keep wearing your *Gimme A NOD!* shirts so that you might hook up with some other kindred spirits. If nobody seems to have missed you too much on the home front, let it progress to dinner and drinks with her and your subsequent adoptees. When all of you are really feeling bold (please note that I recommend a year of small steps so that everyone involved will be appropriately acclimated), I dare you to escape together for an entire weekend away.

After 48 uninterrupted hours of laughter and play, you'll either realize you need to move to a new town to get away from this wacked out woman who won't leave your side or, more than likely, you've found a true friend who isn't guaranteed to always live nearby, but will always have a spot in your sappy little heart.

WHY *IS* IT THAT…I'LL SETTLE FOR BEING A PART-TIME DIVA?

Some of my girlfriends and I recently escaped on the mother of all getaways by spending nearly three full days in selfish bliss. If we continue to hone our skills in resourcefulness and manipulation, our excursions will baby step their way to becoming weeklong and international within five years. And if we're really good, our families will never even see it coming.

Should anyone dare to deny us our annual retreat, we have come up with at least seventeen ways to rationalize it: not the least of which being that we are a heck of a lot nicer to be around after we have been pampered and silly. If our husbands have a problem with it, they can take their frustrations out on L'Oreal's ad executives for not just hiding our roots but reminding us that we are, indeed, "worth it."

This year we girls went so far as to name our sweet escape "Divas in the Desert" and proudly wore matching baseball hats stating as much. Your initial reaction may be to wonder why anyone would want to be identified by a name that implies she is snotty and egocentric. Does it make more sense when I explain that there are twenty-three children between us eight part-time divas who force us to spend the other 362 days of the year as the antithesis of such selfishness?

Somehow I can't picture Whitney, Mariah or Celine spending the vast majority of their days sporting hairdos best described as "surrendered" and counting baby wipes as the primary staple in their grooming process. Our being able to emulate a much-scaled down version of their existence for seventy-two hours sustains our otherwise selfless lives until the next annual pilgrimage to our fountain of youth and sanity.

To best appreciate our determination in pulling off this logistical feat, imagine the challenge of finding a weekend that each of our extended families had free. Every father, grandparent, aunt and uncle was involved in providing care for these twenty-three needy creatures who were temporarily abandoned by their mothers.

I think that most of us had to suppress our feelings of excitement and relief as we said our good-byes so as to not hurt anyone's feelings. As soon as we buckled our seatbelts and awaited our preflight instruction, one particularly astute diva said the words that would become our motto: "It's all about me!" With that on the table, each one of us was aware that we were all out for our own personal comfort, relaxation and entertainment. We were free to pursue our own pleasure, but without treading on that of another diva-friend. Fortunately, this worked smoothly because we were all similarly elated to eat in any restaurant that didn't have booster seats or kiddie menus, tickled to shop without strollers or tantrums, and ecstatic to snooze until we chose to open our own eyes.

We started our first full day with professionally prepared espresso drinks and a trip to the spa. Is there a better way to start the day than having someone grind both your coffee beans and knotted muscles for you? From there, we hit the mall and discovered the figure enhancing benefits of Body by Victoria lingerie. Like an excited child with a new pair of shoes, we strutted out of the shop convinced that our purchases would be a life altering experience. Then it was on to a poolside lunch and some tanning. Despite all dermatological warnings, we know without a doubt that tan fat is far more attractive than its pasty counterpart! Once we were bronzed and bathed it was off to another feeding, and time to shake our aging booties. Not bad for a day's work.

With this group of girls, there is never a need to seek formal entertainment because the eight of us together are quite a floorshow. The more proper ladies at the hotel discovered this earlier in the day while lying in their lounges and look-ing appalled while we good-time girls made cannonball entrances into the pool. In our dementia, we chose to believe they were secretly envious of our free-spir-ited attitude. The result was that most of us spent the better part of that day cry-ing, not because of the slightest trace of sadness, but because we laughed so hard that the tears just came rolling out.

We returned to our families rejuvenated after sharing our latest stories, laugh-ing as heartily as our children, enjoying good food and wine (and the occasional tequila shot) and rejoicing in our togetherness.

Though we cherish these weekends, we're aware that the pursuit of diva-dom should be limited to one week of the year. If we got away with more than that, we might become too wrapped up in the star treatment instead of focusing on the friendships. None of us would want to become so selfish and demanding that we would alienate our friends and end up having to hire an assistant to trail behind us (and our accompanying egos) to mop up the mess of our lonely tears. We'll prevent that isolation by keeping our diva-ness as a part-time pursuit so that we never take those magical weekends of girlfriend giggles for granted.

Yeah. That's why we'll limit it to one week a year. It's all about keeping it real…and has nothing to do with knowing that we'll be lucky enough to extend our escape to four days.

WHY *IS* IT THAT…WE DON'T ALL ASPIRE TO BE *DOMESTIC PARTNERS?*

At the very least, the environmentalists should support me in my plan for same-gender cohabitation since the overpopulation of our planet would certainly be lessened if we all decided to shack-up permanently with a member of our own respective gender. Come to think of it, I'm pretty sure I could count on the support of any woman with ten years of holy matrimony under her belt, as well. But before the extremely "hetero" of you gross out and the homos throw another parade, please know that my master plan does not include anybody's definition, presidential or otherwise, of the wild thing. You see, I propose that we each marry and cohabitate with our closest same gender friend.

What do we do about our more primal urges? I suggest that we approach these needs as we do a fill-up at the local gas station: a once a week visit for the average American, biweekly for those of us with additional drive and monthly for those who tend to be more pedestrian. You see, everybody is a winner with their libidos appropriately satisfied and their day-to-day living spent in domestic bliss.

Imagine, ladies! We would celebrate our union by registering for linens and draperies made from every floral print available, particularly those designed in the un-manliest colors imaginable…just because we could. Our beds would drown in a sea of innumerable pillows with no man around to count them out loud in an exasperated tone as he chucked them carelessly to the floor. (If they knew how much those babies cost, they might treat them with a little more respect.)

There would be potpourri on every tabletop so that we would never have to smell unpleasantness. Come to think of it, though, without those stinky shoes and socks cluttering up the house and our olfactory sense, it might not be as essential as it is now. We could, instead, rely on the fresh flowers and candles that would, without question, rank in importance with food and electricity in our monthly budgets.

We would have two closets of clothing from which to choose, and would always remember to tell each other just how fine we were looking. There would certainly never be a raised eyebrow when we debuted a new outfit. The price would always be a bargain and the fit so perfect we would have to inquire as to if it had been tailored.

Our lives would be pretty and pleasant without suffering from derriere d'toilette in the wee hours of the night, finding razor stubble in our freshly cleaned sink and being serenaded to sleep by the harmonizing of a clan of hogs.

Gentlemen, do not fret, because there are plenty of benefits for you as well! Just think of the fortune you would save by avoiding the cost of windows and curtains in your homes. Practically speaking, it makes plenty of sense since many of you have never bothered opening the ones in your current quarters. After several years of marriage, we broads have finally figured out your childhood fascination with Batman; do your people *ever* crave daylight and fresh air? Before you go getting defensive, embrace the fact that you and your superhero friends could adorn your cave walls with all of the moose and boar heads that you could possibly hunt and gather in a lifetime.

Your little nest would, otherwise, be free of bric-a-brac since nothing without function would be allowed on the premises. That ought to make your biannual dusting job just that much easier. You could, instead, spend your free time affixed to a recliner while smoking a stogie without anyone threatening you to a night of solitary confinement because of your room-clearing stench.

Nor would you have to duck the occasional, but well deserved, slap for bringing home that incriminating box of matches from a strip club with an address that just so happens to be in the same town as your last business trip. For those of you who admire these pole dancing women or the silvery-nude-silhouette variety that you like to believe want to ride you as well as the back of your truck, please pair-up at once. It shouldn't be a problem finding one of these like-minded soul mates since the former are readily found in bars across America and the latter are currently traversing each one of our national highways.

Others of you may find your life partners while swinging and cursing away on the links since, in your hearts, you would rather be there giving away most of your money and free time anyway. This plan of mine would put an end to the painful existence of golf widows who, while genuinely mourning the loss of their husbands to this sport of masochists, spend their lonely days wishing that life insurance companies would legitimize this as an actual loss of life.

Once we had selected our life partners, we more sentimental saps would spend our evenings laughing and crying to programming on the Lifetime network, sans the benefit of your snorts and eye rolls. And, without us around to interfere with your favorite programming, you guys could throw away your remote control and leave your TV permanently parked on ESPN.

Did somebody suggest throwing away the remote control? Over your dead body! That nefarious invention could actually be a tremendous caveat to your all male, all the time tranquility. With two Alpha males on board, who would be the designated driver? Perhaps it wouldn't even matter since you both would have the requisite short attention span necessary to enjoy the perpetual flipping of channels. Nevertheless, I have a hundred dollars on this being a substantial issue at the Bat Cave. After all, one of you would have to be Robin!

Should things ever go sour (and I am not talking about the spore-ridden food in your refrigerator) in your permanent state of male bonding, imagine the luxury of being able to pocket the niceties and tell each other where to go. Later, when you had forgotten or no longer cared about the point of contention, you could sweep the whole issue under the rug and go shoot some hoops.

But if a mess should present itself that was beyond the scope of the broom, what would you boys blame it on if PMS were no longer such a convenient scapegoat? Perhaps you would have to look in the mirror and acknowledge your (vast) share of the blame. Yes, lads, our monthly cycle has been known to magnify an emotion or two, but it has yet to actually create the scenario that called for a hysterical reaction in the first place. Holy truth serum, Batman, I think she's right!

I don't know about the rest of you, but Barb, Jackie, the Tracies and I are off to register…just as soon as we stop for a fill-up.

5

The Seasonal Blends: Light and refreshing when you need them to be, hearty and hot when you're not

WHY *IS* IT THAT…WE CAN'T RE-SCHEDULE OUR RESOLUTIONS?

Okay, okay, we all like the idea of a fresh start, but can we at least be realistic? Perhaps not when you consider the circumstances under which we set these lofty goals. Why is it that they always prove themselves to be as unrealistic as deciding to run a marathon in six months' time when we have recently considered installing a landing at every third step in our home? But when dressed in our finest, complete with a glittery New Year's tiara that makes us feel ever so regal, despite its cardboard composition, and shoes so stylish that they insure we will at some point be on a first name basis with a podiatrist, we feel so glamorous that we feel somewhat omnipotent. Couple this with the consequence of having lost track of how many glasses of champagne slid down our eager-to-be-celebrating throats, and trouble is in the making. It is at precisely this time, in the height of our glamour and slow synapses, that a fellow reveler inevitably brings up the annual "R" word.

I am certainly not advocating any type of boycott of this tradition of setting goals for self-improvement. Announcing your abstention at the stroke of midnight would do little more than label you a party pooper, and have you moved right off the "A" list and onto the "B" for any future fete. My suggestion is simply that you save all planning of your own little self-improvement scheme until precisely 8:00 AM on New Year's Day. You won't find yourself quite as delusional when you are sporting flannel pajamas and a bed-head beehive of a 'do that is trying desperately to cradle a head whose only ambition is to stop pulsating.

I am guessing that any resolution made at this time will be reasonably attainable. "I will never drink again because alcohol is poison." Check. After the recommended dose of Advil and a hot pot of black magic, a few more may even come to mind. I guarantee, however, that you won't be promising yourself to exercise every single day, come what may, knowing that you also need to juggle the needs of your family, work and just-cleaned-but-already-dirty home. After all, two days a week sure beats zero! The same goes for a family dinner. In an ideal world, we would all sit down together for every meal, but work schedules, after-school activities and mom's loathing of the kitchen always find a way to intrude. But, two days a week sure beats zero! If you find yourself gorging on leftover treats, don't try to quit cold turkey, just comfort yourself with the fact that two cakes a day sure beats twenty! Should your issue be one of compulsive shopping 'til you're dropping…all of your hard-earned cash, keep in mind that two maxed-out credit cards sure beats twenty!

Do not fret if you received this warning after the ball dropped and your grand promises were made, for it isn't too late to avoid disappointment. You can still find success if you follow this simple mathematical equation. Take this year's resolutions and divide by two or three (depending on just how good you were feeling at midnight) and get on with it!

WHY *IS* IT THAT…MOTHER NATURE DIDN'T GET A PINK SLIP?

On blustery winter days, I want to don a curly red wig and belt out my off-key rendition of *The sun will come out tomorrow*. I figure that the heavens will receive it as the polar opposite of a rain dance and a protest over the job performance of Mother Nature. She is, after all, the one being I can blame for my wintry funk.

By early February, the frosty chill of winter has lost all its novelty (even here in California) and I am left craving the warmth, color and rejuvenation of spring. If I could just slip that infamous weasel of a groundhog a little something to take the edge off, perhaps he wouldn't get so freaked out by his shadow, and we could permanently shorten the cycle of dreariness that defines winter. On second thought, I don't think even an early spring would be worth the wrath of P.E.T.A.! Perhaps, instead, I should try to schedule a little face time with Ms. Nature for a little chat…one that ought to take place out of earshot of The Big Guy if I ever hope to share his zip code.

Old girl, I suspect you have buried your head in the clouds too long and are unaware of the changes we earthlings have endured this year. Wake-up, Sister! Competition is fierce and there are plenty of folks on unemployment who would be eager to compete with you for the honor of bringing our sad souls a little more sunshine. If you attempt to rebut with gibberish about our water supply, my response will be that if people have been clever enough to find a way to send instant messages around the world with a point and a click, then I'm sure you can find a way to fill our lakes and rivers without having to mess with my hair or require me to visit the car wash. Times are tough, Mother! Be creative! While I'm making requests, let's make sure we stay somewhere between seventy-three and seventy-eight degrees, since anything less makes me carry a sweater and anything more turns me into one.

Mamma Nature, please get over your power trip soon and bestow some warmth upon your subjects and get on with the duties of spring. In the past, this has only required you to provide conditions for growth, but if you would like to retain your cushy career, perhaps you could showcase your multitasking skills by becoming involved with what is actually growing. Because it's not all roses, honey!

While contemplating a leaf-less view and trying to think warm thoughts on a chilly February afternoon, I am reminded of a folkloric song dedicated to spring that plays tribute to all things that are colorful. The first image that came to the songwriter's mind in *De Colores* is that the countryside "dresses itself in color in the springtime." Well, Mother Nature, in my case, the image of the countryside's vibrant rolling fields needs to be downsized to a suburban excuse for a backyard that will, come April, boast color…though probably only one; green—lots of green. In fact, for at least one month per year, the grass actually has some spots that are an appropriate shamrock shade. But, alas, so are the impenetrable clusters of weeds that seem to breed kin faster than the infamously prolific rabbit species. They grow thick and proud and force me to walk with the posture of a geezer when I wage battle with them. Goddess of Nature, I'm thinking your job security would be tighter than a pop star's abs if you could work a little magic here and design some sort of a plan for their extinction.

Before we are forced to go up the chain of command and take our grievances directly to The Boss, I suggest you show good faith in your desire to stay on board by beginning with a rewrite of your mission statement to say something like: "Effective March 1st all weeds and dismal weather will cease and desist. There will be flowers and sunshine for all." And should you find the execution of these duties to be an overwhelming task, I suggest you take a look at Monster.com to see just how tough the competition is.

WHY *IS* IT THAT...SOME LIKE IT HOT?

According to cultural icons Marilyn Monroe and Robert Palmer, *Some Like it Hot*. Well, at the risk of trying to sound like Dr. Seuss, I do not. My theory is that the more northern your heritage, the more you agree with me. If your natural skin color is best described as "lunar," you feel heat like a hound. The temperature rises and leaves you dripping, panting and shedding everything but those extra pounds that further enhance your discomfort. Those of you with skin tones that range from caramel to cocoa sound yummy enough to top my latte, but become unpalatable by daring to ripen just when I have proven myself perishable.

While I shuffle through the torrid summer days at the pace of a sloth, hugging the perimeter of buildings that offer only enough protection from the sun to shade a Hollywood waif or the average kindergartener, you exude an annoying aura of vitality. You jog, frolic in the park and generally bask in the warmth of the midday sun, leaving me to feel like I ought to summer in Transylvania. I would consider relocating if the schools were good and I could abstain from the sucking of blood while still adopting the flowing black cape. After all, isn't a jet-black sheath that creates a slimming vertical silhouette every girl's dream cover-up? I'm sure you agree...unless your cellulite distributes itself less traditionally than mine and winds up on your still visible ankles and face.

The dilemma is that covering up from head-to-toe fits nobody but the Amish's definition of sexy. By coupling the soaring temperatures with western culture's insistence that summer is the sexiest of seasons, I am forced to exhibit vast expanses of clammy skin. And somehow, despite all dermatological warnings, I still believe that "mommy's soft tummy" and arms that often double as pillows look somewhat closer to Hollywood's standard when three shades darker than their God-given and postpartum state.

Regrettably, the tanning process requires spending time outdoors in sweltering conditions that leave me feeling like only the most literal definition of "hotty." Part of it, surely, is the unsightliness of my discomfort. If I could suffer internally, it would be one thing. But no, I have to leave behind a cheek print after sitting too long on man-made fabrics and display a forehead shiny enough to cause onlookers to squint. My armpits, too, feel the need to announce any temperature over seventy degrees. To the deodorant makers of the world, I say test your products on people who actually have auxiliary sweat glands, or stop the false advertising. I listen to your commercials, and would be thrilled to raise my hand if I were "Sure." Well, I *am* sure of one thing...that I blew through your product ten steps outside my front door.

Alas, somewhere within the first three letters of "sexy" lies a word that implies a need for physical contact. Those who know me well (yet didn't pass through my birth canal) wouldn't dare get their 98.6 degrees near this Wicked Witch from the North on a three-digit day. And someday my Munchkins, too, will realize that mom doesn't sic the flying monkeys on them if they avoid skin-to-skin summer contact. One thing is sure: my "no-touchy" policy is great for birth control, but tends to be tough on a marriage. Though my husband hasn't admitted it, I'm sure he was hoping that our summer project of installing central air would make me a little more like Glenda or, perhaps, like some sort of naughty-but-nice little sorceress. Too bad a lady can't tell you which one he ended up with.

Psst! Hey, babe. Set the thermostat to 65. I just got the cape out of the dryer and I'm coming to bed.

Summer in Seussville

I do not like the heat on me.
It makes me sweat, can't you see?
I do not like to stick to the seat
Nor wear repellent and smell like Deet.
I do not like a shiny face
Nor when there's a ring on the armpit place.
I do not like to hate to move
Till the A.C. is on I have no groove.

6

Third Cup Theories:
Where a warped mind wanders
after one cup too many

WHY *IS* IT THAT…WE DON'T SPRAY WHENEVER CHANGE IS IN THE AIR?

It finally dawned on me why David Bowie stuttered the word "Ch, ch, ch, changes" in his aptly named song that, with the help of speech therapy, was simply and victoriously named *Changes*. After all, it's hard to spit out a word that means venturing away from the known and out into the God-knows-what.

The problem is that once you utter the word, you might just have to act on it. And even an aging pooch will agree that it's far easier to rest on one's laurels (or any other horizontal surface) with the tricks he's already mastered than to figure out exactly what the crazy, treat-wielding human is asking of him. *Master, I excel at playing dead. What exactly do you want from me?*

Old Rufus and I both know that the prospect of change is scary, and its execution can be as drawn out as any on Death Row. Frankly, my canine companion will be serving me coffee in bed before I ever take on some of the issues that could leave me sounding like a locomotive before I'm able to spit out the rest of that "Ch" word.

My aversion to change is evident in many aspects of my life, but is most easily spotted in my biweekly jogs around the neighborhood. While some would say that altering your route keeps the workout more interesting, I say that both my head and my thighs need to know when it will end. The few times I ventured down the path not usually taken left me carting around psychological sandbags in addition to the extra pounds I was trying to shed. Slow and steady may win the race, but slow and heavy just want to sit down.

The same can be said for my diet. I know what's too good to be true. While I would be thrilled to believe that the answer to my beefy BMI is a fad diet of cheese and pork products, I know I really need to replace all foods packaged in bright yellow wrapping with those that sprout up from dirt. The problem is, I never quite acquired a taste for those vegetables not found in a standard-issue salad. Plants such as cauliflower, broccoli and lima beans that have been officially deemed "edible" never manage to activate any of the four known flavor sectors on my tongue. Since they don't register as salty or sweet, nor spicy or bitter, I am left to assume that a genetic mutation bestowed upon me an undesirable fifth: the wretch sector.

The problem is either physiological or entirely my mother's fault. After reading studies about introducing new foods to babies, I know that it can take fifteen exposures to new eats before they taste like something a child should swallow instead of launching them from his mouth. I'm confident that my beloved mother stopped at 14. There was enough repetition to make the torture memorable, without ever getting me used to the most noble of side dishes. Nevertheless, there is pride in eating something horrid for the sake of your health and, once you're past the age of twelve, shame in leaving it on your plate.

If I can't bring myself to chew a spoonful of peas (do they count if you swallow them whole?), you can imagine how petrified I am at the latest change I have embarked upon. My husband and I have decided to transplant this old tree to a new location. The problem is that my roots have had thirty-five years to embed themselves in the only land I've ever really known. It's a risky endeavor. With my sensitive composition, the new soil could cause shock and paralysis. And with no familiar landscaping to surround and comfort me, I could fall right over in a forest of strangers. Does that mean I fell at all?

With any luck, the tree…er, I will make my way through the new terrain and find something to wrap my roots around. The new paths won't be easily forged due to those psychological sandbags that will inevitably be packed and moved with our more desirable possessions. But, with any luck, the roots will take hold and I, the toughest thing to transplant, will start to blossom with the first dinner invitation offered by a potential new friend. And if I successfully avoid offending the hostess by rejecting her healthiest side dish, I may just survive and flourish there despite myself.

WHY *IS* IT THAT…YOU THINK SHIRLEY MACLAINE IS SO OUT THERE?

Anyone who knows of Shirley MacLaine's New Age beliefs, and enjoyed the credit card commercial in which she poked fun at herself by making purchases well suited for several of her past lives, knows where I'm going with this. You either think she is a freakish, out there kind of woman or you acknowledge, like I do, that reincarnation helps make sense out of some of our more unexplainable interests and beliefs.

As a teenager, I thought my mom was on the embarrassing verge of becoming eccentric for being drawn to clothing adorned with fringe and feathers. Here was a conservative, June Cleaver of a mom with an entirely too public longing to debut Vegas showgirl attire. I thought (and prayed) she was joking when she explained the cheesy attraction by claiming that she must have been a cowgirl or an Indian princess in another life. Now that I find myself not fitting well within the confines of my own mold, I am beginning to think that, as usual, mom just might have been right.

The seed of discovery was first planted when our oldest daughter was just learning to speak. I became a little spooked when she continually pointed to an Irish Setter in one of her books and exclaimed "King!" Before you go looking for reasonable connections, I assure you there are none. There were no signs of royalty in that book with which to confuse her, nor did we know anyone with a dog that looked even vaguely similar to His Highness.

Had it been a picture of a key that she mistakenly referred to as "king," it would be one thing, but last I checked, the words "dog" and figurehead leader don't have much in common, phonetically or otherwise. If this had all been reversed and she had mistakenly pointed to a picture of Prince Charles and proclaimed him a dog, I could have made sense of it. I could have chalked it up to my doing too much royal watching in her presence, thereby stating my opinions on his canine-esque straying more strongly than I had intended.

King remains one of our family's unsolved mysteries and has made me curious as to how many of us humans find our interests and passions. Some are easy to connect. That a painter has a son who wants to be a sculptor or musician seems obvious; the arts are in his blood. For anyone to desire to become an actor, sports hero, lawyer or doctor is not so shocking either, since these professions are known to bring prestige and wealth. How do you explain, however, the more illogical attractions that guide some of us away from mainstream tracks and our own family background?

Take, if you will, this Germanic looking blue-eyed blonde with a passion for most anything originating south of the U.S. border. While the attraction is in no way scandalous, it simply isn't part of the Gringo norm. Since the path to becoming a Spanish teacher is paved neither in gold nor in stock options, mine was hardly an impacted major in college. There was clearly no cultural pull to the job either, since the salsa always ran mild in my neighborhood. And though my fair-faced family would never spell clan with anything but a "c," there really wasn't a significant ethnic influence in my life until I left for college.

My university years were more diverse, not because of a large heterogeneous student population, but because I chose to spend part of them in Spain and Argentina. But what made me want to become fluent in Spanish, live in these countries and then use my experiences in both to become a self-proclaimed Latina wannabe?

For the record, my allegiance was formed a solid decade before the 1999 Grammy's, when Ricky Martin's gyrating extravaganza turned skin the color mocha into a mainstream staple. And though I do enjoy his music in English, he had me shaking my Spanish speaking bon-bon several years before any of my honey-haired homies knew who he was.

All this leaves me to hope that I could possibly have spent the days of a previous lifetime picking coffee beans in the fields of Colombia until Juan Valdez himself fired me for consuming all the profits. Once unencumbered by work, I was then free to spend my nights shaking it to the warm, Caribbean beats of salsa and merengue.

Psssssst. Shirl, if you're making all that New Age stuff up, don't ruin it for me. I don't want to know!

Why *IS* it that…my hair doesn't inspire musicals?

"Let it fly in the breeze and get caught in the trees.
Give a home to the fleas in my hair. A home for fleas, a hive for bees
A nest for birds, there ain't no words
For the beauty, the splendor, the wonder
Of my…"

—*Hair,* the musical

Oh there are words for *my* hair—limp, lifeless and thin, for starters. But those aren't the lyrics the cast was singing about when the musical *Hair* debuted Off Broadway in 1967, on the very same day I was born. Perhaps it's because I came to life the same day the show did, but I spend way too much time thinking about the seven strands of the stuff that God bestowed upon me. It's probably written down in heaven as one of the great celestial ironies that a near hairless woman would be born at the exact moment this body part was being singled out and celebrated.

When each strand of a girl's hair plays a precise and crucial role during the daily grooming process, there's really nothing to sing about. Instead of belting out a tune and practicing my jazz hands, I must instead save my energy to search for miracle working products and a magician of a stylist who charges me more than a week's worth of groceries.

But for those of us who have never been approached to do a shampoo commercial, the amount spent on regular visits to the salon is anything but an extraneous expense. To put it in terms my husband can understand, I like to use an automotive analogy. Just as my car needs a regular lube and oil-filter change, I need to trim and tint my treasured locks. It's called maintenance. And if done regularly, disaster and great expense are avoided.

I try to explain to him that if a fabulous social opportunity presented itself, and I hadn't been recently coiffed, I would then be forced to either take matters into my own hands while armed with nothing more than junk-drawer scissors, or visit the shaky hands of the beauty-school-dropout hairdresser at the local mall. The other alternative would be to buy a stunning new outfit that would distract people from noticing my shaggy mop. Either way, there's a significant price he'll pay. He will either be forced to cope with a tantrum more hysterical than any he's witnessed in a Toys R' Us, or he'll find a Visa bill for that smoke-and-mirrors of an outfit that will put him in touch with his own inner two-year-old.

The real reason my husband doesn't argue, though, is because he knows that the day I visit the hairdresser is one of the most cherished on my calendar. I go to the salon knowing I will spend an uninterrupted hour in a chair, sipping my favorite brown beverage. *Ahh.* Once seated, I chat or read a trashy magazine that lacks any resemblance to the hard news that leaves me more than mildly hopeless and depressed. After just fifteen minutes, I reach my own state of nirvana. While he may envision such serenity in an ambiance of incense and soothing music, my sense of peace comes, instead, from the pervasive scent of bleach and the catchy opening tune to the Oprah show playing in the background.

Was I this tired when I arrived at the salon or did my hairdresser slip me some scalp-penetrating-something during the shampooing? It doesn't really matter because that head massage felt so good that I'm not sure I care if I've come to this state naturally or not. Probably even better than that feeling, however, is knowing there's a considerable chance I'll leave the salon looking cuter than when I arrived.

So that my husband does not become a source of disappointment for failing to notice, I always greet him with: "Thanks, Hon! I love my new do, too." If I didn't cast this line in search of a compliment, I'd have to spend the next few hours flipping my hair dramatically in hopes of him noticing. I would, then, become increasingly more exasperated that he did not.

If there's anything worse than having my transformation go unnoticed, it's being all coiffed-up and having nowhere to go. It pains me to leave the salon looking my best just to plop my lovely new do on my pillow. For this reason I've learned to avoid evening appointments so that I may get some mileage out of a new style that I'll never be able to replicate. Whether it's a trip to the grocery store or a quick dinner out, I can believe for a few moments that my hair really is something to sing about. *Laaaaaaaaaaaaaa!*

WHY *IS* IT THAT…THE FASHION POLICE FIRE WITHOUT WARNING?

Anyone who spends time with teenagers, as we high school teachers are loath to do, needs a Herculean sense of self…or at least a bionic eye for fashion. Lucky me. I have neither.

During my years as a high school teacher, however, I did have an ear for all the doubts and insecurities my students confided in me privately once class had ended. My Dumbo-sized ears and a generous set of shoulders inadvertently made me into something of an approachable teacher. The comfort many of the students felt in chatting with me, however, soon bit me in my equally proportioned butt and made me vulnerable to the commentary of our City's finest, The Fashion Police.

These junior officers of fashion law honed their wit and skills in observation during their awkward adolescence. The cruelest of the department skewered their peers, perhaps with the hope of turning their venom pro by eventually working for a celebrity magazine. But it's always kosher to direct your wrath at the Hollywood Hoochies since everyone knows they're just looking for the kind of coverage that their clothes will never provide them.

The kinder, gentler students seemed to have different motives. Perhaps they were just attempting to fulfill their community service hours with polite interventions for the sake of their beloved teachers. Their goal was to show us that there was more to life than sensible shoes, khakis and a non-descript top.

Their concern was heart-warming and, if they had understood the art of discretion, their efforts might even have been appreciated. If they could have just whispered an after-class warning instead of sounding the sirens before writing up my latest fashion infraction, I might have been more open to change. Instead, the siren blared and I stood paralyzed like a captured criminal awaiting the cuffs.

One day, while fully engrossed in the presentation of one of my more captivating lessons, a young lady raised her hand enthusiastically. As I looked out at a sea of apathetic faces, I was delighted to see that at least one student shared my excitement for the new concept. After all, it was worth staying up late to create a new lesson if it helped even one student see things more clearly. When I called on her to share her thoughts, however, it was evident that the only thing she saw clearly was that my belt had crept up over the waistband of my pants. I'm sure my disappointment was even more visible than my indecently exposed back skin.

Another time, I used a method straight out of Teaching 101 and insisted that two boys share with the class what they had been whispering about. Imagine my sense of horror upon discovering that they were discussing whether I looked more like The Jolly Green Giant or a green bean in my outfit. Once I recovered from the shock, I actually hoped they decided on the bean. Even while feeling humiliated, I knew that long and lean sure beat Jolly Green! Then again, they could have been thinking along the lines of the Limas.

After a few more years under my unwieldy belt, I actually thought I had developed a personal style that was conservative yet had, dare I say, an occasional flare for fashion. I felt pathetically victorious when I overheard several lieutenants from the local squadron as they whispered that I dressed "pretty cute...for a teacher." There are certainly two ways to take that "compliment" and I chose the only one that made me feel good.

Wouldn't you know, though, that the only compliment given to me out loud that year came on a day that was so cold in my classroom that I overlooked the gross-out factor and put on the cleanest jacket I could find in the lost and found pile in the back of the room. Of course they liked my jacket. It was the one thing they had ever seen me in that I didn't buy myself.

The Chief of Police herself delivered the biggest blow by far. She, my most ebullient student in eight years, rushed up to me as class was about to begin. She said, "Señora, my friends and I were talking at lunch and, please, don't take this the wrong way. We want to get you a Jenny Jones makeover!" This was the final and fatal blow to what remained of the shallow sector of my self-esteem.

If you think I'm overreacting, I ask you to look at the before and after pictures of the next makeover you see. Please notice that they do not arrange these magic shows of make-up and fashion for the average person who could use a little more spice in her life. No. They pick a real dog with a distant glimmer of potential who, with truckloads of foundation and clothes actually purchased in this decade, will no longer scare the viewing audience. It was clear that my personal gauge for what was aesthetically acceptable, as I looked at my reflection in the mirror each morning, must now be chalked up to delusions of grandeur.

Once the bleeding stopped, I vowed that, chic or not, the next addition to my wardrobe would be a flak jacket. Though it did nothing to add to my street credibility, at least it shielded my vital organs from those weapons of esteem destruction.

WHY *IS* IT THAT…THEY SAY 'BEAUTY IS ONLY SKIN DEEP?'

Skin, schmin! Any girlfriend worth her second "x" chromosome knows that beauty covers way more ground than one's skin. After all, hair, clothes and accessories carry just as much beauty clout as a well-preserved epidermis. While mom still insists that beauty is all about your insides, one look at the pages of *In Style*, *Cosmopolitan*, or *Vogue* leads me to believe that our family matriarch might finally be wrong about something. Bless her cotton socks for trying to keep me from having hurt feelings, but I'm old enough to realize that men drool and women flare their nostrils in disgust because of something more than a supermodel's high IQ and dazzling personality. I just have to decide how far I'm willing to go in my quest to activate the boys' salivary glands and the women's nose-crinkling reflex.

There's really no way around the fact that when people ponder beauty, they define it by what is attractive to the eye. Some of the cover girls may very well be dumb and/or demonic, but aesthetically speaking, they've got it goin' on. Those of us who don't are trying to educate ourselves as to what "it" actually is so that we may start "it" up. While in our hearts we know we'll never be the next Cindy, Tyra or Kate, you can't blame us for buying a few of the latest products and fashions with the hope of having our own personal beauty break-through.

Oh, to be au courant! I do admire those changing styles, but mostly from a safe distance. After many years of trial and horror, I have figured out from which fads to abstain. They tend to be those that are overly leg focused because when I stand with my feet together, not even a flea can get past my thighs' defensive line.

How my sorority sisters and I used to giggle at the Greek name bestowed upon me! I no longer remember its English translation but am still haunted by its pronunciation: *you-a-thigh-uh*. I suppose it could have been worse with the strategic placement of an "n" that would have left me with some variation of the "uni-thigh" that hits way too close to home. Need I say that miniskirts and those form-fitting stirrup pants were never my best look?

I finally came to peace with the fact that my body type isn't the muse for many runway-inspired trends. Armed with this realization, I now have compassion for those gals who have either lost all energy to care what might best flatter their body type, or simply don't spend enough time in front of a full-length truth-teller.

While I understand that a big girl's options are limited, can I just say that garments comprised almost entirely of spandex should never be made in anything larger than a size 8? Designers really don't do us double-digit-sized girls any favors by making skimpy clothes readily available to us. While we do want to be fashionable, we do not want to buy something in a delusional moment that will only depress us when it comes time to show a vast surface area of dimpled skin. I'm not asking for their spring lines to consist of muumuus in an insultingly bland array of colors and patterns, but couldn't they make a variation of what the waifs will be wearing that just has a bit of sleeve and more coverage for our self-chafing gams?

Until the designers acknowledge the buying power of a girl who will pay a hefty price to hide the fact that she is just that, we girls have to support one another by giving honest shopping advice. For starters, don't let a girlfriend display her midriff unless she looks, in the flesh, like an airbrushed vision off the cover of *Cosmo*. Additionally, you must shake your friend by her naturally padded shoulders should she try to buy low-rise pants that merely accentuate her back fat. You owe this to your sisters.

Unlike those who think it's better to grab attention from a misdeed than to get none at all, I find it's often better to blend. I accept that my non-descript style will keep me from being featured in any sort of fashion spread. Since there won't soon be a spot for a wide-thighed gal next to the images of Nicole Kidman and Halle Berry in the fashion icon section of my *US weekly* magazine, I'll just lie low and continue with the Slim Fast shakes. After all, the only alternative is to get publicity as the anti-example. Anonymity sure beats being skewered by the clever barbs of the Fashion Police who could then crown me Queen of the Hollywood Ho-down of fashion faux pas.

Besides, I still have plenty of other avenues on which to squander my husband's paycheck in my quest for beauty. The cosmetic counter still embraces me with open cash registers as I continue to buy and apply all of the latest masks, scrubs and creams. Their promise to erase the acne scars, brown spots and the anything-but-fine lines that cover my countenance keeps me hopeful…and keeps the salesgirls from being demoted to the children's department.

I will also keep buying and pouring myself into all of the "Wonder" products that will help me corral all that extra skin into more desirable regions. I will even give that horrendous thong one last chance to stop feeling like the kind of wedgie that could cut a girl in half vertically, all for the sake of being free from those granny-panty lines that were somehow socially acceptable for the first 2000 years A.D.

And, against my better judgment, I will buy several pieces of clothing each season that will, without question, be passé and tight on my not-so-bootylicious assé by season's end. When that fact starts to get me down, I'll just go visit mom and ask her to remind me of all the relatives who are awed by the beauty of my charm and cleverness.

WHY *IS* IT THAT...THE IDEAL TEACHER'S GIFT AIN'T NO APPLE?

During my years as a high school Spanish teacher, I received many gifts of appreciation from the students whose lives I'd touched. Some were kind enough to bring me homemade goodies while others brought castoff apples that had lost out to Hostess products at lunchtime. And those who knew the quickest way to my grade book, er...heart, brought gift certificates to my favorite coffee shop. While I appreciated all forms of thanks and free caffeination, the greatest gift by far was the daily attendance of the class goofball.

The odds had it that in a class of thirty, there would always be one. While the rest of the class greeted my lessons with a blank stare or the always-encouraging roll of the eyes, these few gems made my lesson plans run smoothly and made me smile during my workday. The cooler ones, and the accompanying sea of aspiring wannabes, were too afraid to let loose and enjoy themselves for fear of social retribution.

Apparently, there's an unspoken rule that cool people must appear to be comatose while in the presence of their teachers. While those teachers still employed by a school district might not say it out loud, I'll admit that I had favorites. I simply couldn't resist the ones I didn't have to check the vital signs on. The hearty "¡Hola!" they projected as they entered the room made me know there would be one fewer potential candidates for CPR that day.

One particularly memorable student campaigned relentlessly during the first few days of school for the Spanish name Cállate. This moniker, by the way, is not a name at all but a command to be quiet. Apparently, the name became endeared to him in his Spanish I class because the teacher said it to him so often that it started to feel comfy. His recounting of the origin of his name on the first day of class was, to say the very least, a red flag the size of China. In pondering the challenge that might lie ahead of me, I even thought of trying to pawn him off on another teacher. But it didn't take long to realize that with a name like "Shut-up!" his trading viability was virtually zilch. While he did, indeed, live up to his name as the year progressed, he was also good for many a chuckle.

I saw the first glimmer of his geekdom when he was quick to announce how much he enjoyed the Latin American pop music I shared with the class, while the others merely groaned about it. But the event that would give away his invisible pocket protector was the day he confided in me that, much to his devastation, he had just fallen down in front of two darling, popular girls in our class. He was adorably pathetic to confess that a more paramount audience couldn't have witnessed his clumsiness.

Another day, he and another student stayed after class for some extra help and, somehow, our conversation turned to the *Grease* soundtrack that this silence-impaired boy had in his CD holder. I expressed my disbelief that it could possibly have been the twentieth anniversary of a movie I saw at least seven times in the theater. I even boasted knowing the words to all the songs. I put on the CD and sang along shamelessly until the *Hand Jive* song came on. I was in the process of lamenting that budding signs of senility kept me from remembering the accompanying hand motions when, low and behold, 'ole Cállate started busting all the old moves right in front of another student who could have wiped out any remaining street credibility the kid held on to.

I thoroughly enjoyed and appreciated the fact that this high school student had the guts to be so silly at an age when social acceptance is of utmost importance. I am confident that the world will be hearing from my dear friend "Zip it" as he finds his way into other people's hearts and, perhaps, center stage. I also know that if our current lives were running more parallel than perpendicular, I would seek him, as well as a handful of other goofball students who have brought me so many fun memories, out as a friend.

While the gift of a free latte got me through many tough afternoons, even the gorgeous union of steamed milk and espresso beans couldn't beat the daily presence of a student like "Shut Up" in the life of this teacher.

WHY *IS* IT THAT…IT ISN'T COOLER TO BE A GEEK?

I'll admit that no one wants to be too closely related to the horn-rimmed glasses variety that often comes fully accessorized with a masking taped nose buffer. Nor do we long for high-water pants, French fry station hair or a machine gun laugh. But can we just admit that the nerds of youth seem to have much more fun and, often times, success than the rest of us in post high school life?

I, for one, am willing to bet that Bill Gates was not voted Most Popular by his graduating class, but I'm sure he's now the first alumnus to sign up for his class reunions. On the other hand, maybe he's more gracious than I would be. He may avoid the event so as not to embarrass the Biggest Jock and Most Flirtatious recipients who never left home. That way they'll still be able to hold on to the title of Big Fish in a Tiny Puddle. Whichever approach he takes, one thing is sure…he and the rest of the world's geeks are certainly getting the last laugh.

My own high school days were more of a closet type of nerdy since my friends and I were a bit more devoted to preserving a perception of coolness. Somehow our secrets were never revealed to the voting population and we became our school's cheerleaders and class officers. Our peers must have thought we were cool, but we knew in our hearts that if anyone had bothered to plot us on a spectrum with polar ends labeled "dork" and "cool chick," we would've been just one step ahead of Urkel. After all, we did have our own air band named Menstrual and The Cramps and spent our weekends cruising the streets of neighboring schools with the hope of stumbling upon a party to which nobody cared to invite us.

While my pals and I were undoubtedly dweeby, we had and continue to have so many fun times that the more icy of you are missing out on. We see you driving your convertible BMW while wearing dark glasses and talking with such an air of importance on your cell phone. Don't you ever speak with someone funny? Or is it just beneath you to smile and laugh? Well, we just can't understand you because we're the girls you see performing a one woman concert while we drive in oblivion to our own less lucrative jobs or the carpool line at our children's schools. Admittedly, though, most of us are known to tone it down a notch or ten if we realize you're watching our show. After all, we don't recall you buying a ticket! We still have, even after all these years, a tiny remnant of that old desire to preserve our reputation that makes us slightly ashamed of our goofiness. Once you've left our minivan in the dust and we no longer feel the heat of your disapproving (or, perhaps, envious) glare, however, you can bet that we'll most certainly pump up the volume. Rock on, sisters!

On more rare occasions, usually only when we've swapped our coffees for cocktails, we have been known to lose our public shame and let geekdom reign. Not long ago, for example, some of my friends and I went to play a little pool at one of those trendy little locales where you can break some balls and bust some moves all at the same time. The DJ on duty must have done some advanced mathematical calculations to figure out what kind of music might get a free floor-show started. He picked a winner with us when he let the entire *Saturday Night Fever* soundtrack ride. With pool cues as microphones and some Travolta-inspired moves, we laughed and strutted our way to playing the longest round of billiards known to man. God only knows what the onlookers thought, but I'm confident we had even more fun being freaks than they had while watching and laughing at our freak show.

If an average Josephine's experiences aren't enough to sell you on dumping your cool act to join the ranks of the good time geeks, perhaps I can entice you with the opportunities for fame and fortune in which goofdom can play a role. It won't actually bring you stardom, but once your talent gets you to Tinsel Town, your nerdiness will be what endears you to the hearts of Americans.

Take Cuba Gooding Junior, for example. His Oscar winning acceptance speech has been the most moving one made during my lifetime. The excitement and emotion he shared with us that night made me a lifelong fan. If he had accepted his award with the usual dry, dispassionate speech I would have only remembered him as "that guy from *Jerry MacGuire*". After his Oscar night effervescence, however, I remember him by name. Go, Cuba! Go, Cuba! Go, Cuba, Cuba, Cuba!

Without further a due, it's now time to pay homage to the Prince of Passion, the Earl of Enthusiasm and the most captivating character of cinema, Mr. Roberto Begnini. Remember him? While the visual of him actually making love to everybody he offered to bed upon receiving his nominations and awards in 1999 is not entirely beautiful, life in his company must truly be. Despite the fact that I only understood half of what he said, I cried every time that man gave an interview. To see someone that exuberant about what he does is entirely contagious and inspiring. If we all had just an eighth of that energy for our work, oh what a world it would be! Somehow, though, I think I would have been arrested if I'd mimicked his provocative invitations in the presence of my high school students. Please share more of your talent with us, signore, and I, for one, will start studying Italian so that next time I'll understand everything you say. Capice?

While the rest of us should not try to replicate such naturally flamboyant and emotional styles, we can find our own individual way of celebrating our passions and successes. I will always be happy for someone who experiences victory, but will stand up and jump for joy for those who have shown their vulnerability by sharing how much it means to them to find such success. If you are too cool to do a little jig or shout out with glee, we fans would just as soon give your gold medal to the silver medallist or your Oscar to the first runner up. To share a little wisdom from the Homestead High School cheerleading squad, "you've got to want it to win it and we want it more!" We spirited girls weren't afraid to show it, either, unless, of course, we became more interested in a cute boy on the other team…but I digress.

The less famous of us won't be winning any statues or necklaces made of large chunks of precious metal, but we can still apply the example to our own lives. Let's force ourselves to do things in our every day living that we usually feel like we need to hold back until we can comfortably free ourselves from inhibition. My own personal goal is to not stop wailing my tone deaf tunes as I pull up to a red light, to leave the globs of blue glitter nail polish on my fingers just the way my girls proudly paint it for me, and to learn how to dance with abandon without the assistance of liquid courage. I will try my darnedest to conquer these few remaining fears of geekiness without being haunted by one of those horrendous chants of youth "N-e-r-d spells nerd. You are a big, fat nerd. All right. All right."

Isn't it time to correct that old adage that erroneously states that "blondes have more fun" by informing the world that it is we nerds who do?!

WHY *IS* IT THAT…THE APPLE DOESN'T FALL FAR FROM THE FAMILY TREE?

I am strung higher than any garland decorating our national Christmas tree. For that reason, my husband has been trained to announce his presence by stamped-ing through our house like a pachyderm…or risk being greeted by the type of shriek that heralds the arrival of a masked, ax-toting psychopath.

You would think I was a government informant the way I respond to surprise. When I go to the movies, I must restrain myself from dropping to my knees and shouting "shots fired!" when an actor so much as sets down a glass. The backfir-ing of a car is enough to send me patting myself down in search of bullet wounds and my heart pumping like the newest generation gas dispenser at Chevron. And, yes, I know I'm a perfect candidate for decaf.

To better understand my anxiety, I examined the nearest branch of my family tree. If my mother could have any say in the matter, ours, by the way, would be a potted, indoor Ficus variety. That would ensure that the vast majority of bugs and varmints would have no opportunity for contact. Lord knows the perching of a single housefly could be enough to leave her leafless for an entire season.

But since mom never wanted her neuroses to interfere with providing me with life experiences, she challenged nature by becoming a Girl Scout leader. She flourished in the crafts and creativity, but eventually had to take us to the woods. It was practically written in her job description!

The daylight hours proved uneventful, but as we young girls giggled into the wee hours, a scream sounded off from a nearby tent. I am quite sure that one of our fellow campers used the experience to write the original screenplay for *Friday the 13th*. That camper was clever enough to use the melodrama to make millions while the rest of us are still too scared to pitch a tent to this very day. As every-one scrambled about like ants after the first spray of Raid, one thing was certain. A fellow scout was dead or, at the very least, dismembered. When it was *my* mom who surfaced from the tent in the middle of a psychotic episode with every one of her limbs still connected to the appropriate socket, I knew embarrassment was imminent. At least the source of her horror turned out to be a cricket, and not some measly mosquito, inside her sleeping bag.

My branch of the tree is far more resilient. Everyone knows that an unex-pected baby lizard is a far better reason to require a paramedic's paddles than any old cricket. So while two inches of nature nearly caused mom's death, it took a full four to threaten my longevity.

My girls and I were leaving the house just on time for a ten o'clock appointment. It was a beautiful summer day, made even more glorious by the fact that my daughters weren't battling it out like Serena and Venus for a change. Couple that with the fact that my appointment wasn't for one of those bi-annual teeth scrapings, but instead an indulgent morning of massage and pampering, and you'll understand my euphoria. (Lest you think I'm spoiled, though, please understand that these days of decadence come about with the frequency of the Olympic games, and are just as equally celebrated.)

My oldest daughter opened the car door. She froze. She panicked like the two generations before her. "There's a lizard in our car!" she screamed repeatedly. I did a quick survey to see who was going to have to take charge of this situation. Since I outranked both the five and the seven year old in title alone, I resigned myself to the responsibility.

The wheels of panic were spinning fast enough to make me a contender in the Tour d' France. Lance, Schmance! I grabbed a broom and swept and danced about like Dick van Dyke in Mary Poppins. Nothing. No four-legged movement whatsoever. It was time to go and I had a decision to make. Should I risk my daughters' lives and drive while dodging the advances of a frightened reptile or miss my quadrennial massage?

Let me tell you. I twitched, itched and hallucinated phantom lizards throughout my journey and arrived to the spa just in time to enjoy, like never before, the aromatherapy and soothing touch of a professional.

The bravery I demonstrated for the sake of my massage, I mean my daughters' image of me, should warrant a fresh new bud on my limb of the family tree. With any luck, this one will more closely resemble cactus than Ficus.

WHY *IS* IT THAT...WRITERS AREN'T BORN WITH EXTRA LAYERS OF SKIN?

It never occurred to me why I lost interest in the invigorating morning wake-up scrub provided by my beloved loofah. Its cavernous pores and scratchy bits were simply left swaying from the shower head during the morning cleansing ritual until, one day, a cleaning frenzy sent me disposing of all unnecessary clutter. But when was it that my faithful exfoliator rendered itself extraneous? I can't pinpoint the exact date, but am confident that when the terms "query" and "S.A.S.E." could still send me to the dictionary, it was still being employed with vigor.

By advanced calculations best left to technology, it is reasonable to deduce that I stopped all frenetic scrubbing about the same time the editors started doing it for me. During the first few months of the submission-rejection drill, I was nothing short of raw. My tender flesh would not have withstood even the gentle rub of a towel endorsed by Martha. At least that is why I assume I spent the entire first week as a rejected writer without bathing or leaving the house. It does nothing, however, to explain the vast quantities of potato chips I consumed while consoling myself over the demise of my almost career. When you consider the salt content of America's favorite junk food, I should be celebrated as a hero for daring to place them anywhere near the open wound that was my entire being.

I continue to suffer from boomerang-itis as my submissions find their way back to me, addressed in my own familiar scrawl. Those dastardly self-addressed stamped envelopes conk me on the head, trying to penetrate the deep layers of the denial process that keep me from pursuing a more validating career. Perhaps the next flying stick will hit deep enough to make me realize that my dream of filling the void left by Erma Bombeck is about as likely as my bulky frame being devoured by the infamous super colony of ants.

I sense that my mail carrier feels the imminence of this awakening. He brings up news bulletins of UFO's circling around New York City, the publishing capital of the world, and then heading back out west. He also alluded to pursuing advanced training for situations that can be more volatile than an encounter with an unrestrained guard-dog. While his boss, the Postmaster, may claim that his people carry pepper spray to keep protective pets at bay, I think we writers know better. We may very well be the reason these guys have been known to go postal!

Once, before he knew any better, my faithful mailman tricked me into thinking I would have a rejection-free day. After relishing in my relieved reaction, he dared to wallop me with a sucker punch by revealing a hidden manila envelope from behind his villainous back. After gasping in horror, I decided he needed a lesson in non-verbal communication. Frankly, if all human gestures were as effective as the one I demonstrated, we writers might just be rendered obsolete.

This manila-letter day led him to explore some more subtle techniques to avoid the ugliness that could have landed us both on the Jerry Springer Show. I refer to his new tactics as the "drop and run" and "subtle tuck" methods of delivery. He thinks he is clever, but is obviously not a postal valedictorian. For, who would have thought that the sounds of a turning doorknob and the suction release of weather-stripping could make a postal employee disappear from your porch faster than he would at a union mandated break-time?

The one reprieve my postman received from the wrath of this scorned writer was the day he was clever enough to begin our encounter by handing me the box containing a much anticipated pair of shoes that had been on backorder. Then, when I was just three steps into my happy dance, he fished into his bag for the always-recognizable envelope. The letter, of course, was as well received as any containing anthrax. That is, until I remembered my adorable new shoes…at least there is one antidote to the pain.

My only fear is that a few more years of accustoming myself to the "Dear John" letter of writers will either leave me devoid of any emotion or still insane but rivaling Imelda in my collection of footwear. Though I am not yet at the stage of even wanting to control my impulse to murder the messenger, I could, due to the high volume of rejections received, conceivably become so blasé as to recycle them with the rest of the junk mail. By then, my entire outermost layer of skin will be calloused beyond the scope of any loofah and may just need to be polished with an industrial sander.

7

The Perils of Parenting:
The add shot years

WHY *IS* IT THAT…I DIDN'T JUST HIRE A SURROGATE?

In this age of convenience, why on earth do most women bother to bear their own children? My theory is that the horrors of childbirth are purposely hidden from us girls until we have already gotten ourselves in that age old "predicament."

It is undeniably fun to conceive a baby and, for the most part, the little ones *are* little bundles of joy in the outside world, but can't we avoid the ugliness in the middle? After all, we aspire to hire out all of life's other pesky chores. But, hands down, when pondering the parts I haven't repressed, the birthing process outranks cleaning the toilet and grocery shopping in the company of two small children on my list of things I don't want to be an expert about.

And I was as prepared as any Girl Scout worth her badges! I attended class, had my bag packed a month in advance and had the baby's room ready to go. Then I waited…and ended up begging to have the creature removed from my being.

When my husband and I finally checked into our luxury suite at the hospital, we frolicked about taking final pictures of me in my *Hee-Haw* overalls. Then, sometime during twenty-three hours of nothing but poking and medicating, it ceased to be fun.

The doctor suggested a C-section and attempted to refresh my memory as to what the procedure entailed—to very little avail. What I did remember from Lamaze class was that many women seem to lose all composure when push comes to push harder. I aspired to do better…with a little help from vanity and a whole bunch of drugs. The determination to avoid being one of those wailing psychos was replaced by big-eyed fear as I was wheeled off to a sterile room where far too many people in masks scurried about. The dignity I was striving for became impossible as my arms started flapping involuntarily like a startled chicken while I was informing the anesthesiologist that he was my very best friend.

I certainly wasn't feeling that kind of bond with my husband and my mother who had just eaten a chocolate bar in my presence, which resulted in a scene right out of *The Exorcist*. Well, to be perfectly honest, my head didn't spin around, but the projectile aspect was very similar.

Several hours after my less than speedy delivery, the baby and I struggled through the first feeding. *Ahhh*. At last it was time for a little shut-eye. But within minutes, the gruffest nurse you can imagine walked in and stated with great authority that it was time for me to stand up. Yes, you heard me, stand up. I had not slept, eaten nor been caffeinated in over thirty hours. A squirming, squealing little creature had just sucked my boobs for the first time and every layer of my abdominal wall had recently been cut…yet I needed to stand up right then.

It was then that I decided that the videos presented at childbirth class had actually been censored for the sake of our species. The truth would only lead to our extinction! But, between you and me, the psycho wailers whom I mocked for their lack of restraint were refined enough for an invitation to the palace when compared to me, the prehistoric roarer whose anguish echoed throughout the sixth floor.

But now that the physical wounds have healed and the trauma has been reduced to a clever tool to manipulate my children when they misbehave, I realize that my initiation into motherhood was sadly fitting. While my wedding day was spent bidding adieu to single life by sipping champagne, eating fine food and dancing with abandon, this next rite of passage proved itself far less romantic…unless, of course, there can possibly be a happy ending to something that began with bile, blood and a beast-like bellow.

WHY *IS* IT THAT...THE TOLL ON MOM ISN'T DEDUCTIBLE?

Have you ever noticed that most women start to focus on their inner beauty about the same time their first child is born? Please don't be so naïve as to think that we girls are trying to change the superficiality of the world for the benefit of the next generation. Heck no! Girlfriends are just grasping at straws! After nine months of gestation and the first three nights of sleep deprivation, mama knows peace and love are about all she has left.

In the wee hours, when a cries sounds off and eventually registers with my delightfully dormant brain, I start the mourning process for my *sleepus interruptus* by at first denying the problem. It might not actually be denial. It could just be a moment of hope that my husband will hear the cries and leap out of bed before I have to. But lets face it ladies, most men have the good fortune/nerve to sleep in a coma like state that makes that moment of hope very unrealistic, even laughable.

I'm sure that plenty of renowned pediatricians would put me in parent counseling for what I do with our two girls. When they awake at night, the experts say to console them briefly and leave the room. I don't know whose children they tried this approach with, but our feisty females could challenge the best of them! Oh, my! A girl *can* carry on! So I have learned not to waste any precious R.E.M. time. I just let the first to awaken sleep with us and, later, jump in bed with the inevitable second screecher. This bed, by the way, is twin-sized and my daughter attaches to me like Velcro on one side as the wooden bed rail cuddles my other. To a well-rested adult, this game of musical beds is, of course, stupid and wrong. But in the middle of the night, I am not as concerned with doing the right thing as I am with getting right back to dreamland.

After several years of enduring this routine, I am confident that at least one other human understands my pain. Much to my bitterness, as previously stated, this other person is unequivocally not my beloved husband. This icon is one who should be included in my prayers for being the king of exhaustion delay...the almighty founder of Starbucks! I can only assume he received his inspiration from a similar state of exhaustion. Let's just say I've had enough lattes to delay mine for another thirty years. So why am I still cranky?

The lack of good sleep certainly brings out some aesthetic issues as well. Mirror, mirror on the wall, who in the heck is that sunken, rodent-eyed shrew looking back at me?! Before having those sweet babies, I never understood the importance of concealer. Now I don't let anyone who isn't related by blood or vows see me without it!

On those two-cups-to-wake-up days, I feel a special bond with our dog, Holly, whom we bought from a breeder and embraced as our first child. We were shown a picture of her studly father and were quite impressed with his taut and perky good looks. When we inquired about the mother (I avoid breeder speak so as to reserve that special "B" word for when referring to supermodels), they allowed us to meet her. Holly's mom, bless her heart, looked like she had given birth to one litter too many. The droopy eyes, the listless stance and the stringy hair that I remember from that day haunt me on those increasingly frequent helluvadays when I look in the mirror.

So it won't come as a surprise to hear that, some seven years ago, I discovered that underneath this shell of a haggard pooch lies one loving (though not yet entirely at peace) mom.

WHY *IS* IT THAT…KIDS CAN'T JUST STAY IN DIAPERS?

Saying good-bye to diapers is a glorious day both environmentally and financially, but be careful what you wish for! I don't like to change a ten-wiper any more than the next mom, but potty training is just a swapping of evils. It is like having to make a fire escape plan for a building every time you go out. From the moment your toddler sounds the alarm, you have approximately thirty seconds to find the nearest public restroom. If you don't find the quickest, most direct route, you will indeed get burned. Frankly, battling flames might be easier than peeling layers of wet and stinky clothing off of a fidgeting child. And if, in all the hoopla of trying to leave the house, you neglected to bring a change of clothes, forget about it. Abort the mission and head for home!

While many experts say not to try and rush your toddler into toilet training, there is one external pressure to conquer it: preschool. By June, we had our little one enrolled and as mentally prepared as a three year old can be for the beginning of school in September. The only remaining hurdle was consistency with the potty. Even those relentless days of summer were passing by so quickly that I was starting to panic. It was time to brave the garage in order to dig up the notes and books I saved from Psych 101. Had I realized during those narcissistic days of youth how important behavior modification would be once a small child was in my life, I am sure I would have given that information a more prestigious and more easily accessible place both in my memory and in the garage.

Since our daughter spent her first verbal year saying "no" more times than any mom would say in a lifetime of trips down the junk food aisle of the grocery store, reverse psychology seemed like the obvious first step. I must admit that it took award-winning acting to pretend that it didn't matter to me that she peed all over my clean floor instead of in the potty that was just three feet away! As clever as she is, it didn't take her very long for her to figure out that I was far from indifferent to her haphazard displays of urination. Perhaps the first clue came when she noticed the way I jumped so quickly for the disinfectant! The whole act was blown for sure when my dry heaves accompanied the clean up of the other kind of mess. You know, the one that really inspires potty training. I could just see that look of recognition in her spunky little eyes. If she had possessed vocabulary that reflected her attitude, I am sure she would have said, "Like this really doesn't bug you, Mom. Do you think I was born yesterday?"

Since, Lord knows, there is no aversive therapy imaginable that is worse than walking around in a pile of your own feces, we thought the next logical step to be the employment of positive reinforcement. Lest you think we are idiots, I must explain that we began this whole process by overwhelming her with the praise and encouragement best understood by a professional cheerleader, but to no avail. We needed a desirable external stimulus, one with a bright colored exterior coating that only revealed its milk chocolate center when placed in your mouth (not in your hands!). The ever-delicious M&M approach worked wonders! I can't say that most dentists endorse the sugary method as readily as I do. Nor can we be sure, at this time, what long-term effects a chocolate addiction will have on her health. We can only assume, due to evidence found on her family tree, that the price she will eventually pay will be one of pant size.

My angst continued for two more page flippings of the calendar. Then, finally, it was more of a routine than a fluke that her cute little cheeks would perch proudly on her potty seat. I would like to think that my college education played some role in the making of this milestone, but the truth is that ninety-five percent of her success can be attributed to her physical and emotional readiness and, much to the dismay of the medical community and her mother, America's favorite confectioner can claim the other five.

WHY *IS* IT THAT…NEW PARENTS AREN'T SENT HOME WITH "SWEEPERS"?

You're probably thinking that I am the only woman in America who hasn't been visited by a sales rep from Kirby when, in fact, I am proposing something far more sinister than a miracle-working vacuum or electric broom. If you spend your evenings sprawled and in a daze on the family room couch, you may soon understand my scheme. Since my husband and I spend most nights too exhausted to do anything productive (or carnal, for that matter) once the kids are in bed, we tend to get our thrills through primetime programming. While experts argue that this medium curtails creativity, I beg to differ. Television inspired *this* woman to hatch a plan to help every gal in the trenches of this dress-down profession called motherhood.

While watching one of the many drama series that deal with shady, subversive types, I was introduced to the concept of "Sweepers." They are basically the bad guys' janitors who have a knack for erasing all evidence of wrongdoing. Actually, it is more than a knack since they operate with the understanding that someone else will be sweeping up *their* remains if they fail to execute a proper clean-up job. So knack, schmack…these guys are the ultimate survivors. They perform or they die, it's as simple as that. And their services would be the perfect addition to the free samples of formula and diapers that accompany each new mom out the hospital doors and into her forever-changed life.

I sure could have used my own live-in "Sweeper" last week when my four year old decided that a few dashes of "fairy dust" would be a perfect addition to her artwork. The magical dust, contained in an ornate silver necklace with a delicate little vile dangling in its center, was a gift from her grandmother to be sprinkled about whenever she needed a little insurance that her dreams really would come true. God bless Grammy for keeping a childhood fantasy alive!

While the little flakes were plentiful, it is safe to say that the entire bottle of wishes would have been used up long before reaching the end of the first aisle of a Toys R' Us outing. And this mom's skeptical, mess-averse eye never got past the fact that fairy dust bears an uncanny resemblance to over-the-counter glitter…and is, therefore, just as challenging to pick up.

But in a moment of caffeine-induced stupidity, I gave the green light to incorporating the glitter, er, fairy dust into my daughter's picture. I am not sure if she hoped that a little magic would transform her work into something reminiscent of Monet, or if she is simply as jaded as her mother and saw it as a convenient source of everyday pink glitter. Whatever her intent, she pushed the cork inward (ensuring that the vile would never close properly again) and got about her business. After fewer than three minutes and seventeen shakes of dust, the artist gave an approving nod and was ready to move on to other mediums, abandoning the project *tout de suit*.

And there I was, left with one of motherhood's many ethical dilemmas. Do I dispose of the now uncontainable vile of mess or try, once again, to be a Montessori mom who lets her child flourish through the process of discovery? Judge me all you want, but that necklace was promptly buried under banana peels and coffee grinds so that I, the evil perpetrator, would be guaranteed to never see the look of horrified disbelief in the eyes of a betrayed preschooler.

While my daughter quietly disassembled another room, it dawned on me that even one flick of fairy dust left behind would remind my daughter of the world's most annoying accessory item. Panic set in. She was guaranteed to be back within minutes with some sort of request and things were bound to get ugly. It was, without question, time to employ the kind of chemicals that leave fish floating at the surface of our water supply and a sponge capable of exfoliating oatmeal from a cereal bowl three days forgotten. Once appropriately armed, I scrubbed like a criminal, determined to avoid doing some parental "hard time" by giving my little live-in forensics gal nary a fingerprint to work with.

Today marks day three of a successful yet draining round of effective housewifery. Both the frantic scrubbing and fear of being discovered made the whole cover-up process an exhausting one that would truly be best left to gangsters. But should the evidence ever surface during a random fieldtrip to the dump, I console myself that the courts will go easy on me. While I confess to acting without remorse, my actions were not at all premeditated. It was a crime of passion. I was momentarily obsessed with removing unnecessary clutter and soil from my floor. I simply had no choice since my parting gifts from the hospital did not include a "Sweeper"…nor, for that matter, a Kirby.

WHY *IS* IT THAT...MORE MOMS DON'T MAJOR IN CHEMISTRY?

Before you go turning me in to the local law enforcement, please know that my quest for knowledge about chemical reactions has nothing to do with concocting illegal substances to get me through the type of day a pot of coffee can't put a dent in. I'm simply a pacifist in pursuit of just one moment of peace. And by the way, I've seen your children at the park and it's clear I'm not the only one who could benefit from a few more hours logged under the tutelage of a professor in the 'ole chem. lab.

Yep. Aside from Richard Pryor, nobody needs a better understanding of chemistry than us moms.

Rather than focus on creating a compound that would leave me with the vacant stare of hypnosis, this mom is looking toward a specialty in interpersonal chemistry that would ensure the opposite reaction. I do this with the hope that such knowledge would leave me with a pulse and some functioning brain waves at the end of a play date that didn't at all live up to its name. And until I pursue such coursework, I will set a realistic level of expectation by booking weekly "fight dates" for my girls.

Just as coffee and cream are perfectly compatible when left to mesh atomically in my just-awakened mouth, my youngest daughter and her friend are a thing of beauty when left to their imaginations and a jungle of a backyard. (We keep it unkempt, of course, for the sake of their play!) But add a hearty dash of arsenic or a school holiday for my eldest, and things are bound to get toxic.

It is as if the hierarchy of the jungle is out of whack. The monkeys screech. The birds flutter in a panic. The elephants stampede through my living room. And once the dust settles, my bulging eyes are left to witness two Simbas battling over the title of Lion King.

I almost wish one of the little animals would hump on the leg of the other so that dominance would be decided once and for all! But since that type of parenting can lead to therapy for all concerned parties, I have yet to vocalize these innermost thoughts.

Since even a speaking Barbie knows that most important scientific discoveries were made after multiple failures, I am undaunted by our latest mishap. Last week's experiment, despite a careful analysis of variables, proved especially fallible. Yet it enabled this rookie scientist to reach a conclusion just minutes into what ended up being an interminable afternoon of exclusion and whining. The results were clear: Taylor + Sarah is NOT equal to Tori + Marin.

Just as my scientist forefathers Newton and Einstein before me, I will persevere. I will continue to formulate and test new hypotheses by inviting newcomers to the house, hoping that we will eventually find a workable dynamic. A little interpersonal Feng Shui, if you will. And, in case the next arrangement is equally successful at setting the lab and the nerves of this increasingly mad scientist ablaze, I might actually resort to moving the furniture around with the hope that ancient Asian philosophy can do for me what my bachelor of arts degree could not, and calm my savage little beasts.

WHY *IS* IT THAT...MOTHERHOOD IS MESSY ENOUGH TO LEAVE SCARS?

Provided that you're usually of the loving, PTA variety, you can easily repress nearly any heinous moment in motherhood...and, with a careful study of statistics, be sure your kids do, too. The way I see it, if you're working with a 90/10 saint/psycho ratio, your chance of being blamed for your children's future unhappiness is next to nil. With those numbers, your parenting missteps should lead only to the type of emotional wounds that scab nicely, without leaving unsightly scars to remind the children, and you, of your glaring humanness.

Should therapy still be chic when the kids are grown, your conscience will be clear. Your "A" average in parenting will assure you that their free-associations with the word "mother" won't lead them with world-record timing to "dearest." The only time the ten percent will get you into trouble is when you pull a normal mom's version of a Madeline Notsogood and have your failure archived at each and every one of the major television networks...or branded, like mine, as a puncture wound on your forehead.

Please let me rationalize...er, explain. One of the many buttons my youngest daughter learned to push at a young age is the one that continues to raise my blood pressure faster than data traveling by fiber optics along the information superhighway. It's a trait normally attributed to redheads, but apparently works for blondes, as well, when they're not too busy having all the fun.

My little girl moves up the frustration scale from zero to 60 like a high-end import with a prestigious hood ornament. Only this one's a lemon. Once she hits 60, things go wrong, really wrong. Her engine catches fire. Gaskets get blown. Things are generally overheated. The real problem is that my ride is parked right next to hers. If she goes up in flames, so do I. The ensuing fire could propel both vehicles to Baghdad.

For the record, I am not a redhead either. And the irony of my anger over raising my hot-blooded mini-me hasn't escaped me entirely. But for God sakes, she starts it.

Just last Saturday we battled from nine to five, what would be a full shift in a job that actually has a daily beginning and end. I was ready to either clock out or clock her. To say she was as uncooperative and antagonistic as Saddam Hussein during a weapons' inspection isn't quite a fair comparison...to Iraq.

My final unreasonable request of the day was that she tidy up her room before bed. She put her emotional pedal to the metal and headed straight for a brick wall. As I bent down bitterly to speed up the clean up, I made my first disastrous error. I went head to head with her Garden Fairy, whose mere existence is a painful reminder of my lackluster parenting, as it was purchased for the sole reason of silencing my whiny child during a trip to the hardware store.

I wouldn't, therefore, have appreciated the fairy's aesthetic charm even if she had been planted appropriately as a cheesy addition to our outdoor flowerbeds. But because of my daughter's penchant for decorating, the little delight, perched atop a three-foot stem, was sandwiched between the mattress and footboard to sway like a dashboard hula dancer each time there was any movement on the bed. My fumblings, exaggerated for drama, caused the metal post to swing back and smack my furrowed brow. The pixy's hooknose then promptly buried itself into the thin layer of flesh that protected my cranky cranium.

With all the maturity of a two-year old, I taught that $5.99 nymph a lesson. I slammed her down so hard that our family now knows the origin of pixy dust. Those fairies work their magic by tossing the remains of their enchanted peers who have made the mistake of running into a mom who has temporarily lost her sense of humor. Actually, the lesson was probably lost on the fairy in her pulverized state, but my daughter apparently learned a doozy. When I looked up from my tantrum, there she was with her lip extended in devastation. Before dissolving into tears, she wisely stated, "just because you're mad, it doesn't mean you can break things, mom."

And if that weren't humbling enough, one look in the mirror proved that I would not soon forget my failings. Especially since the mark left by a hooknose fairy bears an uncanny resemblance to the shape of an "L" when carved into your forehead.

WHY *IS* IT THAT...NO ONE DEBATES THE ETHICS OF THE REPLAY BUTTON?

I hope with all my heart that the decision to invent and install the replay button on each and every child-friendly boom box in America was made after as much passionate debate as the cloning of Dolly. After all, shouldn't all parents be more concerned with maintaining a shred of sanity than truly caring whether or not all little lambs look like the one Mary had?

I beg the misdirected protesters to take on my worthier cause. After all, a thinking parent should have a hard time viewing cloning as a negative since, at the risk of sounding fascist, there are some irrefutable perks to homogeneity. If, for example, we could count identical sheep when trying to fall asleep as we try to suppress an emerging to do list that rivals Santa's, we'd be able to go from zero to R.E.M. in seconds flat. As it stands now with the subtle nuances of pelt coloration, we're just too distracted to nod off. We can't help but stay awake until the scandalous black one makes her appearance like crazy Aunt Lucy at the annual family reunion.

Surely no one will champion my cause, though, without my acknowledging the real fear, which is, of course, that once Dolly comes out with her wool in all the right places, the cloning of humans will be next. I say so what? As long as they design some type of filter to weed out the Aunt Lucys of the world, why not?

From personal experience, I know it would be far more harmonious around my house if I lived with a slew of mini-mes. I would be assured of spending my days with creatures that valued cleanliness and tranquility, and who detested fighting and music marketed to people under the age of 30. Let every lamb chop taste the same and every child be the very reflection of her mother and we'll all be able to save our feet to picket for the really important issues...like the assaults on our sanity.

The decision to let children control their musical destiny was clearly made before I had an opinion on the matter. Now that I'm a mom of children who are increasingly and frustratingly more literate, and can't be duped by my insistence that the letter "a" makes only the sound favored by Seuss in "The Cat in the Hat," there is no disguising the fact that "replay" is an actual word that means to have your favorite music spew from your pink speakers until mother blows a gasket.

It is evident to all that I, like Seuss' anal retentive goldfish, do not like it "not one little bit." Yet my children remain baffled as to why something they find so positively delightful can elicit such an explosive reaction in yours truly. How, they wonder, can the repetition of the two simple words "Up, up, up. Oh, oh, oh" a mere 3,477 times each day be enough to unsettle a woman who claims to live and breathe for their happiness and well-being?

They look at me with the same concerned and questioning eyes of a puppy halfway trained on a new trick. They sense that my blood has been transfused with French Roast, but clearly can't comprehend why. They watch me percolate until I burst with steam, and then run to protect their little sanity busters from the reach of a woman who suddenly shows her family resemblance to Aunt Lucy.

On occasion, however, when pumping decaf through my ventricles and feeling repentant for some of my outbursts, I try to balance out their future memories of our days together. I recently thought to bond with them musically while doing something special for our troops. I suggested we burn a copy of all their favorite songs to send to the American soldiers. We worked with enthusiasm, feeling like involved citizens for doing our small part. When we were done, the kids were tickled with the prospect of entertaining the troops, while I found my satisfaction in providing a non-violent means to torture the Fedayeen.

Regardless of our differing motives, we all felt warm and fuzzy from the experience. The kids were bathed and put to bed smiling by a mom with a smirk that, to the eyes of an innocent child, looked just like a reciprocated sign of genuine bliss. Despite my ethical lapse, I went to bed mentally logging this day as one of the good ones. Then, before I could redirect them, those peaceful thoughts segued to a flock of sheep in a full-blown Broadway version of another household favorite, The Macarena.

Alas, even with all the progress in science, there's still no antidote for karma.

WHY *IS* IT THAT…WORDS DON'T CONTAIN CALORIES?

You would think the embarrassment of a single public word eating would be enough of a deterrent to stop us from saying aloud that which should never even have been thought. But since some of us are slow in learning our lessons, perhaps there should be a caloric toll for each word we consume. Since my pants are feeling tighter while just pondering this, I imagine the more vain of us would be quick to install some type of filter that diverts the flow of absurdity from the vocal chords down through the intestines where it really belongs. If only I had discovered the filter years ago, my words of wisdom could have exited out the appropriate orifice…instead of humiliating me.

One particularly memorable verbal binge took some four years to digest and must still be costing me calories today. (It's either that or the Thyroid!) I had just been married under a year and was of the perfect age to think I knew it all…and was quick to judge those who didn't. I actually prided myself in being the department's young hipster at our school. But the even sadder truth was that in a crowd of my contemporaries, I was far from trend setting. So far, in fact, that any trend I was embarking upon had long since rotated to the other hemisphere, and left me in the dark. But when surrounded by the polyester-clad teachers who still employed the ditto-making machine, I was practically *Sex and the City*. The smugness I felt showed in my walk and, regrettably, in my talk.

So when it was time to carpool to a meeting off-campus, I gathered all the maturity a twenty-three-year-old me could muster, and agreed to squander away my street credibility by accepting a ride in my colleague's minivan. After spending at least five solid minutes pondering why anyone would ever drive such a geeky car (250 calories), I gave a furtive glance in both directions and ducked into the shuttle.

Inside, there was a virtual picnic strewn about that mini-Winnebago, none of which I would have eaten in my most dire moments of hunger. Had she no pride? From fast food wrappers to fermented cups of juice and carpet reminiscent of a beach whose sand came in the form of crushed cereal and crackers. Yuck! I don't remember how I expressed my surprise, nor do I want to. All I know is that my wide-eyed survey had to cost me the intake of a Big Mac super-sized meal deal. With sundae.

Seven years later, the lesson continues to haunt me each time it is my turn to drive. Though I intend to tidy up each time I exit my little taxicab, the children and their urgencies tend to take priority. So I am left with adhesive leather seats, Dalmatian-like carpet and bits of petrified bagel shrapnel that prevent the seat belts from fastening. Oh…and very little pride.

My friend's minivan would have been prize-winning if compared to the chuck wagon I tool about town in. And, just to complete the meal, I have finally accepted that our next car will have to be one of those sexy eight-seaters with sliding doors. We will start haggling with the dealership as soon as I pay off my recently ordered filter.

WHY *IS* IT THAT…I'M ALWAYS CAUGHT DOING THE PARENTING DRIVE OF SHAME?

You know your calendar is a little tight when your children are actually annoyed by yet another rushed visit to the type of restaurant that is unworthy of even a single star rating. Hearing, once again, the words *"I already have this toy."* after the kids glance with ennui into the greased-stained bags containing their sad excuse for supper should be reason enough to send us parents into nutritional and time-management counseling. The truth is; if we had any real pride, the very first time we heard those words should have sent our tires screeching as we threw the old minivan into reverse, in search of a refund. Nevertheless, we're back again, visiting the land of shiny sustenance for the second time in a week.

The more health-conscious of you may not understand, but we frazzled and frumpy types know that the average toy rotation schedule for such establishments is every seven days. So if they haven't moved on from Tigger to Pooh, sound the parental alarms! Our children are technically overdosing on "food" that will never qualify for even the tiny pointed part of the nutritional pyramid. A few more visits, and the family schedule won't be the only thing feeling tight.

While I am busy enough to depend on the local burger joint to fill the void in my children's bellies, I am not quite stressed out enough to be guilt-free for doing so. Perhaps if I added the role of PTA President to my list of commitments I would be taxed enough to get over the shame. But could I ever really be proud of allowing my children to acquire a taste for food which, should its accompanying toys continue to board the family arc two-by-two, will guarantee a solid "H" (for husky) behind their pre-teen pant size?

The attraction to fast food starts out for the children as a toy thing…and should really just stay that way according to reports on obesity. But if, because of the convenience factor or your own penchant for fat and preservatives; you want your kids to tolerate such grub, you must train them early. Before their taste buds can discriminate. This could be proven if we could ever encounter a modern day cave dweller who had somehow made it to the age of eleven without previously ingesting a kiddie combo meal. Is there any doubt that his first bite would result in a violent spit take? You, too, have experienced this if you've ever made the mistake of eating a take-out burger within twenty-four hours of having savored a honest-to-goodness homemade one. Several things surely became clear:

1.   There isn't much actual beef in a fast food burger.

2.   You have never been more thirsty…or bloated.

3.   Your pants are nearly as tight as the sensation in your chest and your "to do" list combined.

4.   You have the breath of a carnivorous scavenger and, potentially, the limited life span, as well.

Fried and reheated animal parts taste bad and smell worse, yet are a convenient (if not necessary) evil in a life full of soccer practice, dance class and homework. So my family joins the other "billion served" and takes its humble place in the drive thru line. I secretly hope that the only people who recognize us there are other guilty parents waiting their turn to broadcast their super-sized family order for the entire world to hear. I fear that high tech monitors will someday serve the additional purpose of photographing license plates to identify fast food V.I. P.s. Though surely, if the warbled voice on the other side greeted me by name or asked if I wanted "the usual", the shame would weigh in heavier than a Big Mac half way through the digestive process…and might just get me subscribing to *Cooking Light* magazine.

Once the window-to-window transfer is complete, we head home for a private gorging of fried fare. As I wind along the familiar path to our house, I can't help but hope that the neighborhood children and their vigilant parents are in for the night. Especially the ones whose houses routinely boast the proud aroma of real food wafting out the open windows…and into my conscience.

As I round the final corner, hoping to sneak inside undetected, I am almost always met with witnesses to one of my most flagrant parental flaws. I give a friendly wave and repeatedly press the button to the garage door opener. But just when I think I'm safe, one of my little passengers rolls down her window to boast her good fortune. Yes, just moments before, the very same meal was as exciting to her as watching me talk on the phone, but apparently the smell of grease has primed her taste buds…or she is purposely trying to tarnish my mother-of-the-year façade.

Whatever my daughter's motive, her gloating forces me to bow my head as I am caught, once again, during the Parenting Drive of Shame.

WHY *IS* IT THAT…TEACHERS SPELL "MOTHER" E-N-A-B-L-E-R?

I am tempted to look up the definition of "mother" in the dictionary, but I'm afraid to find in print what I saw too many times in action as a high school teacher. I know what the description should *really* read: **moth-er** (*muth'er*) n. female parent who protects, nurtures, but also enables offspring to the point of dysfunction and suffocation. Amen! We love our children so much that we want to protect them from each one of life's difficulties, even though we know the only way to really learn a lesson is the hard way.

My heartstrings are pulled beyond their capacity for elasticity each time my little ones are one step closer to realizing the world isn't always a nice place. When a big playground bully shuns or intimidates my daughters, I have to talk myself into a Zen-decaf mode to avoid the impulse to bust some chops! These, I hope, are natural maternal impulses.

The problem starts when we delude ourselves into thinking our child is always the victim and never the "perp" (*NYPD Blue*-speak for perpetrator). With my intense desire to not be like one of those parents, I find myself going too far to the opposite extreme. I'm usually the first to believe that my two kittens have been the first to let down their claws in any given catfight. It must be my own personal backlash against the overprotective mother bears I virtually needed to tranquilize in order to teach their cubs some lessons about life and responsibility.

On those joyous occasions when I had to call a student's parent due to acts of deception or blasphemy, I nearly broke into song when the parent began by saying "Oh, no! What has he done now?" or "She is going to really regret having done that!" Yesssssss! One less battle to fight! It is, of course, good to trust and believe in your child, but not when there is evidence to the contrary.

Once I spoke with a parent who actually believed her child would not cheat even though I had taken a cheat sheet from her during a test. Did mama bear honestly believe her daughter was holding it for someone else? Or did she think it was a sinister conspiracy concluding in my placing the crib notes under her paper? I invited Mother Grizzly to come down to the school for a bowl of honey and a viewing of the evidence. Nonetheless, she was determined to have faith in her whelp and went so far as to say that it was her daughter's word against mine. I think I finally made some progress by explaining the concept of motive to her. I told her I had nothing to gain or lose in this situation by telling a lie while her daughter would suffer grave consequences if caught cheating. It made me sick to have to explain to a grown woman that teachers don't get involved in education to mess with kids' minds and futures. I begged her to take that into consideration when deciding whom to believe. Tough call!

Another gross enabler arrived at my classroom door within an hour after I had accused her son of cheating on his final exam. When the student in front of him got up to get the other half of the test, her sly little fox of a son leaned forward, studied the other boy's test form and bubbled five problems in a row without looking at his own test questions. Just to make sure my eyes were not deceiving me, I watched this process two more times. I, then, passed the boy a note that instructed him to turn in his test and informed him that he would be receiving a zero on it.

When the bell rang, the boy must have sprinted to the payphone to dial 1-800-PROTECTME before his next final started. His "attorney" was at my door in record time in order to regain control of the situation. She had instructed her client to report back to the alleged crime scene at 1200 hours, upon completion of his History exam. Despite her passionate opening statements, I informed her that I would not have accused her son of cheating had I not been sure of his guilt-iness. She informed me that she knew her son would never lie to her, but if he did (nice logic!) she would know by looking him in the eye. She was going to wait in the hallway for her son and they were going to discuss what had transpired. If her son would deny having cheated, she warned me that she was going to take this up with the Judge (a.k.a. the principal).

These two took a thirty-minute recess to formulate their plan of attack. I gathered things would be interesting since it shouldn't take more than a minute to profess your innocence to your own mother. They entered the room looking appropriately sheepish and the boy confessed he had cheated in order to pass the class. I told him I admired his honesty and then began to explain the consequences for cheating. Mother bear quickly lost the demeanor of professional legal counsel and suddenly began to roar. She had the nerve to ask me what kind of a message I was trying to give her son about the benefits of honesty. I delicately informed her that she could be proud that her son was not a liar, but he still was, in fact, a big, fat cheater. Puhleez, woman! I can just hear you now: "Officer, don't arrest my son! He only kidnapped and tortured these people, he didn't kill anyone." Honestly!

Now that my own daughters are of school age, my commitment to be enabling-free is being put to the test. And, if I may say so myself, I am setting an example for mothers everywhere. Now if you'll excuse me, I have to run my daughter's forgotten backpack up to the school. While I'm there, I simply must have a chat with her teacher about the "excessive talking" comment on my girl's report card. Surely I can make Mrs. Williams understand that if her lessons were more engaging, my daughter would be far too engrossed to talk. Duh!

WHY *IS* IT THAT...WE CAN'T ALL CARRY BLANKIES?

Shhh! Don't tell anyone our family secret. Our daughters are old enough to be ashamed of their bond with their blankies, but still crave the comfort provided by the soothing union of satin and flannel. I would have already put the two of them in therapy, if it weren't for my memory of Charlie Brown's sweet buddy Linus who carried his everywhere as a continuous source of comfort and security.

I'm sure our girls, too, would drag their blankies around as constant, bacteria-ridden companions if they wouldn't be mocked right off the playground. Just imagine how a first-grader's street credibility would plummet if she actually included her cherished "Silkie" in her recess frolicking or after-school play dates.

If you have yet to experience the phenomenon first hand, believe me when I tell you that the schoolyard has no place for self-esteem! If a child is fortunate enough to arrive to school with a healthy supply, there are plenty of bullies out there who are ready to rid her of it...even faster than they snatch the coveted classroom ball from her sweaty palms. Yep. One false move on the blacktop and a kid might as well beg her mother to home-school her.

Yet, as a mom, I wish my girls could stash those delightful satin sheaths in their desks for a quick fix to sustain them through scary math tests and encounters with playground bullies. They just couldn't get caught! One alternative might be to leave the revered rectangles with the school nurse and call them "medicine"...which they truly are.

The problem with my pathetic scheme is that I am no risk-taker...and this would be one perilous endeavor. My plan would be right up there with the X Games, really. For if my girls were caught in the office by their peers mid-cuddle, I would have to start boning up on the fine points of reading, writing and arithmetic. And let me just say that if I thought home-schooling were an attractive option for my girls and me (okay, mostly me), I would already own a complete selection of ceramic holiday accessories to wear around my harried neck. So until I am ready to sacrifice my own sanity, I will have to convince myself that my beloved children stock up on enough squeezes and brushes across the cheek between the hours of bath time and breakfast to fuel them throughout the day.

I can't really blame them for their fetish since I have been known to sneak a few swipes of Silkie's smoothness across my lips when the girls join us in bed for a morning snuggle. It feels so good that it has me wondering why we moms don't keep one for ourselves. After all, motherhood requires a woman to take on the hardships of her young as well as those of the adult world. Heck! We might just need a blankie big enough to convert into the likes of a circus tent in order to protect the whole clan from life's little tough spots and all-out tragedies.

To a child, a blankie is at its best when consoling her through a bad dream; when mom and dad are snoring away down a long, dark hallway, oblivious to her needs. But to a parent, a blankie would weather most of its wear during the reading of the morning paper. Blankie's presence, emotionally speaking, would provide us with comfort and reassurance while, physically, it would serve as some sort of industrial strength paper towel to mop up the tears we shed when reading about the worst the world has to offer.

Though not as monumental as the contents of the headline news, we could also find solace in our blankies when our children face life's more mundane hurdles. Will she be invited to Mary's birthday party? *2 cuddles.* Will she run off the stage in the throws of a panic attack during her dance recital? *3 cuddles.* Will her new teacher set the stage for a lifetime love of school? *10 cuddles.* Is her mother obsessively neurotic about her daughter's rites of passage? *79 cuddles.*

But before I hit the Web to find an exact replica of the cuddly little cloth that serves as a panacea for the little lights of my life, I have just one thing left to consider. *Did Linus really turn out okay?* Because I wouldn't want to find out the hard way that Big Brother found some creepy correlation between adults who like snuggling inanimate objects and some sort of perversion. To be on the safe side, I will delay my purchase until they start marketing blankies to tenderhearted parents.

Until then, I'll just continue to seek my comfort in the hot brown contents of a grown-up-styled sippy cup that serves as a pacifier for parents on the go.

Epilogue

By now you're surely due for another cup. It's okay. I promise.

While coffee won't soon be named as an official sector of the well-balanced food pyramid, we all know that our emotional needs are just as important as our physical ones. That second cup is guaranteed to get you through two more dirty diapers, a newly discovered wrinkle, cooking dinner for four finicky eaters, and the comments made by a spouse who seems to have lost every penny of his common sense.

Besides, if you drink your coffee with plenty of steamed milk, like I do, it has to count for at least one serving of dairy!

About the Author

After eight years of teaching high school Spanish, Shana Moore "retired" to spend more time at home with her husband and two young daughters. When not spinning around like the Tasmanian Devil, she ponders parenting's many joys (think unbridled laughter, spontaneous declarations of love, play dates that don't end in carnage) and horrors (think unexplainable fevers, rigor mortis tantrums in toy stores, and play dates that *do* wrap up in haste due to blood and screams).

She hopes that each chapter of her *Caffeinated Ponderings* will leave you with both a smile and a sense of validation. Whether you have a slight addiction to coffee, an irrational hatred of supermodels, or enough training in domestic peace-keeping to qualify you for federal employment, she assures you she has it all covered!

Shana's writing has been published in The Almaden Times, The San Jose Mercury News and in a wide variety of Web sites.

To subscribe to her *Fresh Brew*, order *Caffeinated Ponderings* merchandise or schedule a coffee break at your local bookstore or coffee shop, please visit: http:// www.caffeinatedponderings.com or contact Shana directly at shana@ caffeinatedponderings.com

0-595-30377-3